TRAILRUNNINGGUIDE
TO WESTERN WASHINGTON

OVER 50 GREAT TRAIL RUNS

MIKEMCQUAIDE

SASQUATCH BOOKS
SEATTLE

Printed in the United States of America
Distributed in Canada by Raincoast Books, Ltd.
07 06 05 04 03 02 01   6 5 4 3 2 1

Cover photograph: Brian Bailey
Backcover photograph: Mike McQuaide
Interior photographs: Jay Drowns: pp. vii, 18, 22. Joe Lalonde: pp. 1, 5, 8, 11, 14. All other
    photographs by the author.
Cover and interior design: Kate Basart
Maps: Marlene Kocur
Copy editing: Heath Silberfeld

Library of Congress Cataloging in Publication Data
McQuaide, Mike.
    Trail running guide to western Washington : over 50 great runs / Mike McQuaide.
        p.   cm.
    Includes index.
    ISBN 1-57061-273-0
    1. Running—Washington (State)—Guidebooks. 2. Trails—Washington (State)—
Guidebooks. 3. Washington (State)—Guidebooks. I. Title.
    GV1061.22.W2 M37 2001
    917.97—dc21   00-052267

Important Note: Please use common sense. No guidebook can act as a substitute for experience, careful planning, the right equipment, and appropriate training. There is inherent danger
in all the activities described in this book, and readers must assume full responsibility for their
own actions and safety. Changing or unfavorable conditions in weather, roads, trails, snow, water-
ways, and so forth cannot be anticipated by the author or publisher, but should be considered by
any outdoor participants. The author and publisher will not be responsible for the safety of users
of this guide.

SASQUATCH BOOKS
615 Second Avenue
Seattle, Washington 98104
(206) 467-4300
books@SasquatchBooks.com
www.SasquatchBooks.com

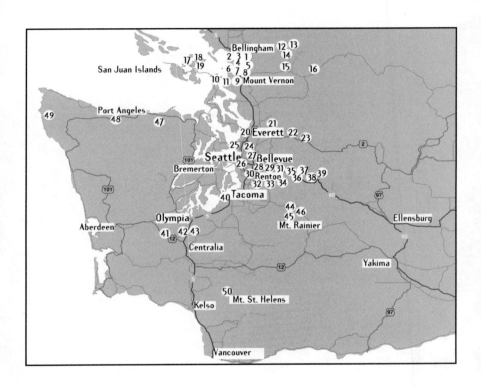

San Juan Islands

Bellingham 12 13

17 18
19

2 3 1
4 5
6 7 8

14

15

16

10 11 9 Mount Vernon

Port Angeles
49
48
47

21
20 Everett 22
23

2

25 24
Seattle 27 Bellevue
101
26
28 29 31 35 37
30 Renton 36 38 39
32 33 34

Bremerton

101

90

97

40 Tacoma

44
45 46
Mt. Rainier

Ellensburg

Aberdeen
Olympia
41 42 43
12

Centralia

82

Yakima

12

8

50
Kelso Mt. St. Helens

97

Vancouver

Contents

BELLINGHAM / MOUNT VERNON   1
1. North Lake Whatcom   1
2. Lookout Mountain Towers   4
3. Lookout Mountain Intestine   7
4. Lake Padden   11
5. Hemlock Trail/Raptor Ridge   14
6. Chuckanut Ridge-Lost Lake Loop   18
7. Blanchard Mountain Loop   22
8. Squires Lake/Alger Mountain   25
9. Little Mountain   28
10. Heart Lake-Mount Erie Loop   31
11. Whistle Lake   35

MOUNT BAKER HWY / HWY 20   39
12. Hannegan Peak   39
13. Chain Lakes Loop   43
14. Scott Paul Trail   47
15. Baker Lake   50
16. Cascade Pass-Sahale Arm   53

Acknowledgments   ix
Introduction   x
The Growth of Trail Running   xii
The Art of Trail Running   xiii
About This Book   xix
How to Use This Book   xx
Route Descriptions   xxii

SAN JUAN ISLANDS   56
17. Mountain Lake to Mount Constitution 56
18. Mount Constitution/Pickett Loop   59
19. Cascade Lake Loop   63

EVERETT   66
20. Spencer Island   66
21. Mount Pilchuck   69
22. Wallace Falls State Park   72
23. Iron Goat Trail   75

SEATTLE / BELLEVUE   79
24. St. Edward State Park   79
25. Discovery Park Loop   82
26. Washington Park Arboretum   85
27. Mercer Slough Nature Park   88

TACOMA / OLYMPIA   134
40. Point Defiance Park   134
41. Margaret McKenny Loop   137
42. Capitol Peak   140
43. Millersylvania State Park   143

MOUNT RAINIER   146
44. Ipsut Creek–Spray Park Loop   146
45. Camp Sheppard–Forest Shelter Loop 150
46. Wonderland to Panhandle Gap   153

OLYMPIC PENINSULA   156
47. Elk Mountain   156
48. Spruce Railroad Trail   160
49. Ozette Trails   163

MOUNT ST. HELENS   167
50. Loowit Trail   167

Resources   173
Race Calendar   176
Index   178
About the Author   182

I-90 / SNOQUALMIE PASS   90
28. Wilderness Peak Loop   90
29. Cougar Mountain Ring   93
30. Squak Mountain Loop   97
31. West Tiger 3   101
32. West Tiger Three-Summit Loop   104
33. South & Middle Tiger   108
34. Tiger Mountain 6/12 Summits   113
35. Mount Si   117
36. Rattlesnake Mountain   120
37. Snoqualmie Valley Trail   124
38. Melakwa & Pratt Lakes Loop   127
39. Kendall Katwalk   131

Acknowledgments

First off, I want to thank my wife, Jennifer, and son, Baker, who are my sun during the day, my moon and stars at night, and the air that I breathe all the time. Their patience and support in putting this book together were invaluable to me. I also want to thank the following individuals and organizations for lending me their expertise and for showing such generosity in doing so: Doug McKeever, Ron Nicholl, John Hastings, Don Kardong, Richard West, Tim Schultz, Wayne Berry, Craig Bartlett and Steve Roguski at Fairhaven Runners, Scott McCoubry at Foot Zone Capitol Hill, South Sound Running, *Northwest Runner* magazine, and Montrail, among others. Babysitters Margaret Gerard and Lynn Herink made finishing this book a reality when it didn't seem that I'd have the time. Finally, thanks to Joan Gregory and everyone else at Sasquatch Books for making this book a reality.

Introduction

I've been running the wonderful trails of Western Washington for more than a dozen years now, so when someone asks me what's so great about trail running, you'd think I'd have no problem coming up with an answer. But I do. A real problem. You see, I have so many reasons—and more reasons the more trails I run—that I don't know where to start. Should I start with how running on a forgiving dirt trail surface is so much less jarring to your body than running on roads, how trail running feels almost like a soothing massage for your feet, ankles, knees, hips, and back? Or maybe I should start with how you don't have to worry about cars, buses, motorcycles, and trucks while you're running on trails. How the air you breathe is a lot cleaner and you can let your mind wander. How when you're running trails in a rhythm, it's like you're flowing in a dream-like state, becoming one with your surroundings. Maybe I should start with that.

Of course, I need to talk about how trail running combines the best of both mountain biking and hiking. Like mountain bikers, trail runners travel relatively fast, covering a lot more ground and thus seeing and experiencing more than hikers do in the same amount of time. But like hikers, trail runners are permitted pretty much everywhere, whereas almost all of the great trails in national parks, wilderness areas, and national forests are closed to bikers.

Then again, maybe it's the scenery you experience while trail running that makes this sport so great. I've run across moraines and tickled the toes of icy blue glaciers, found myself in lush forests so dense with sky-kissing firs and cedars that I've had to practically slow to a walk because it was so dark. I've run across Mount St. Helens' volcanic Blast Zone with the mountain's gaping mile-wide crater to my right and Spirit Lake and its zillions of downed trees to my left. Almost every time you run trails in Western Washington, you find yourself in the middle of some natural, awe-inspiring wonder.

And then there's the wildlife. One time when I was running on Chuckanut Mountain, I came around a bend and surprised two immature barred owls chowing down on their after-school snack. One took off like a shot through the trees while the other flew to a branch 15 feet above me, where it bobbed side-to-side and hissed at me in obvious agitation. I'll never forget that round fluffy face with its black stone-like eyes shooting daggers at me. If I'd been walking, the owls would've heard me and left long before I arrived. I come upon moments of sheer magic like these almost every time I run up and down wooded trails.

And I can't forget to emphasize the ridiculously high fun factor of this sport. There's nothing quite like running wild through an evergreen cathedral forest, leaping over logs and rocks, splashing through creeks and puddles. Few things make you feel more alive than running a winding, roller-coaster single-track trail that slaloms through deep, dark woods. Few things, that is, except running a ridge-top trail that overlooks a zigging, zagging river and a stratovolcano that's almost three miles high. Or running along the Pacific Ocean where the sound of waves crashing upon sea stacks is almost deafening. For me, trail running is more like playing than anything else. There's a sense of adventure to it, especially when you're running a trail for the first time, with no idea what's just ahead, when every turn and twist reveals something new and wonderful.

And of course, trail running is a great all-around body workout. Not only do you get the same aerobic benefits that you get from road running, but because trail running often requires quick maneuvers to avoid roots and downed tree limbs, it improves balance and strengthens muscles often neglected when running the roads. Trail running also gives you an upper body workout from having to counter all your lower body maneuvers.

On top of all that, trail running is an easy and inexpensive sport to get into. If you can run roads or hike, you can run trails—all you need is a pair of running shoes. (They don't even have to be trail running shoes, though such shoes sure help a lot when you get into more challenging terrain.) You don't need any fancy-pants equipment and you can run pretty much anywhere there's a dirt path or gravel road. No lift tickets to be purchased, no required technical gear that runs into thousands of dollars, no reservations to be made, no equipment that can break down—just a desire to have fun and a sense for adventure, that's all.

As you can see, there are so many reasons why I love trail running that when people ask me why, I never know where to start. So I usually end up stuttering around a lot until they get impatient waiting for an answer. And then I blurt out something like "Uh, uh . . . I just think the shoes are cool."

That's why I decided to write this book. To let people know why trail running is so great and to offer a few tips on how best to enjoy it. And also to let others know about all the fantastic places to run in Western Washington.

The Growth of Trail Running

In recent years, as increasing numbers of outdoor enthusiasts have headed for the backcountry, runners have followed suit. A 1999 survey by the American Sports Data, Inc. research group reported that 6.2 million Americans identified themselves as trail runners, and the Outdoor Recreation Coalition of America (ORCA) reported a 38 percent growth in the number of trail running enthusiasts between 1998 and 1999.

Five years ago, only five companies made trail running shoes. In 1999, at least twenty-two offered shoes made specifically for running off-road. ORCA reported that from October 1998 to September 1999, sales of trail running shoes alone amounted to more than $95 million.

While exact figures for the number of trail runners in Western Washington are unavailable, the increasing numbers of entrants in local trail races give some indication of the sport's growing popularity. But despite this upward trend, books on Pacific Northwest trail running have yet to be written. *Trail Running Guide to Western Washington* is the first book geared toward trail running in the region.

The Art of Trail Running

Getting Started

Newcomers to trail running should ease into the sport by trying fairly tame trails. Begin with a combination of running and walking, gradually increasing the running portion while decreasing the walking. Because running trails can result in various twists and turns of the knees, ankles, hips, and other joints, using strengthening exercises for the lower body is a good idea. Consult with experienced trail runners at your favorite running store or health club for specific exercises.

Also, while trail runners of all levels are advised not to run alone, this is especially important for newbies to the sport, who aren't familiar with the challenges inherent in trail running.

Negotiating the Ups and Downs

Certainly trail running shares a lot in common with road running, but there are significant differences. Expect to run slower on trails because their surfaces are so varied, often obstacle-riddled with rocks and roots and marked by abrupt and sometimes extreme ups and downs. Because of this, trail running also requires greater balance and coordination than running on roads. It requires a different kind of concentration too. Runners need to look ahead on the trail to watch out for potential hazards and sudden turns. Have a light footfall and keep your hands slightly in front and low to catch yourself in the event of a fall. Lift your feet a little higher than normal to keep from catching on rocks and other obstacles.

When running uphill, shorten your stride and try to maintain an erect posture. Leaning forward can hurt your back. Lower your hands so that you can use your arms to "drive" up the hill. Speed-hiking and walking are legitimate uphill options and won't get you kicked out of the trail runners' brother- and sisterhood. Everybody does it. Walking is just part of trail running and provides a great opportunity to eat and drink.

When running downhill, take short, quick steps, rather than long strides that cause your foot to slap at the surface. Lift your arms higher and keep them slightly out to the sides. Scout ahead—pick your line—and look for the clearest route down. Your feet tend to follow your eyes. Again, lift your feet high. Bellingham's Doug McKeever, who's finished more than fifteen 100-mile races, visualizes that he's kicking himself in the butt as he runs downhill.

On especially technical downhills, he recommends a skipping motion for getting down quickly and safely.

Mud Running

When you know that your route is likely to be riddled with mud and puddles, lace your shoes tighter to prevent the dreaded shoe suck and plunge
right through the center of the muddle. Don't run around puddles, as that
only widens them and damages the trail.

Hydrating

For trail runs of an hour or more, carry water. A rule of thumb is that for every
fifteen minutes of running, you should drink five to ten ounces of liquid. Of
course trails don't usually have water fountains on them, but luckily, trail runners have available to them a wide variety of hand-strap bottle holders and
hydration packs (backpacks or waistpacks with refillable water bladders that
hold up to a gallon of fluid). Most waist and backpack holders also come with
pockets, great for carrying keys, food, cell phones, and extra clothes.

Water is fine for shorter runs, but if you plan on being out for a while,
sports drinks that replenish carbohydrates and provide electrolytes are recommended. Again, a number of these are on the market. Because of the preva-
lence of giardia, a nasty parasite that lives in creeks, rivers, and streams,
drinking untreated water is a bad idea. If you must drink from a creek or lake,
pill the water with iodine tablets or use a lightweight filter or water purifica-
tion system. Several companies now offer filtering systems that screw right
onto the top of a water bottle.

Eating

Trail runs often last several hours and so eating on the run is important. A
wide variety of sports gels and energy bars are available, which provide excel-
lent sources of quick-burst carbohydrates. On long runs of say, three hours or
more, some "real" food such as sandwiches, fruit, gorp, bagels, Fritos, pretzels,
Slim Jims, etc. is mighty tasty, provides needed calories, sodium and more, and
is worth stuffing in your pack. Experiment to find out what works best for
you and when you find it, stick with it.

Clothing

For the most part, trail running doesn't require a separate wardrobe from your
regular running or hiking clothes. Materials such as polypropylene that wick

moisture away from the body work best for keeping you comfortable and safe. Wearing damp cotton clothing in chilly or windy temperatures is an invitation for hypothermia. A wide variety of lightweight, technical clothing that offers breathability while also keeping you dry is available. Given that this is the Northwest, lightweight rain jackets or vests made of a polyester microfiber are a good idea. Check your favorite running or outdoors store to see what's the latest and greatest.

Shoes

As for shoes, regular running shoes work fine if you only occasionally run trails, especially not very technical ones. However, if you want to get more serious about running in the wilderness, you'll probably want to pick up a pair of shoes made specifically for running trails. They offer a more aggressive tread for added grip on climbs and descents, a toe bumper for protection against pesky rocks and roots, and a wider base to cut down on ankle rolls and twists. Most of these shoes are quick drying for those frequent puddle plunges, and more and more companies are coming out with shoes featuring Gore-Tex uppers for increased protection from the elements. Some trail shoes also come with an underfoot shield that extends the length of the foot to prevent stone bruises. Above all, make sure your shoes fit. You don't want your feet to be slipping and sliding in your shoes while you're switchbacking your way through the forest.

To keep out mud, pebbles, dirt, and other debris, consider low gaiters that fit over the tops of your shoes and cover your ankles.

Weather

Northwest weather can be highly unpredictable, especially at higher elevations. An old salt once told me that above 5,000 feet, there's the potential for winter every single day of the year. He's right too, because he told me this on a summer night when we were huddled in a tent at the toe of Mount Baker's Easton Glacier during a raging snowstorm that featured 30mph winds. And of course, all elevations offer the potential for rain. For longer runs at low elevations and all runs at higher elevations, carry a windbreaker or light rain jacket, wind pants, a hat, gloves, and weatherproof matches.

Hypothermia

If a runner becomes so cold and/or wet that he or she is shivering uncontrollably, has slow or slurred speech and loss of coordination, hypothermia could be setting in. Hypothermia is a condition wherein the body cannot generate enough heat to maintain normal body temperature. Other symptoms of this life-threatening condition include fumbling hand movements and dulling of mental functions. Unfortunately, a person who is hypothermic is usually unaware that he or she has the condition—another good reason not to run alone.

Treat hypothermia by doing the following: Get the person out of the rain, cold, and wind immediately. Remove all wet clothing. Because hypothermia victims are often dehydrated, have them drink plenty of fluids. Get them indoors as soon as possible but remember that gradual re-warming of the victim is advisable. Re-warming that is too abrupt can strain the hypothermic person's heart.

To prevent hypothermia, know the weather conditions and forecast, and always carry extra clothes.

Altitude

Because a number of the routes included in this book take place near 5,000 feet or above, the effects of altitude are certainly something to consider. Although acute mountain sickness is not likely below 8,000 feet (the highest trail in this book tops out at just over 7,000 feet), runners on some of the mountain routes will probably experience increased heart and respiration rates, particularly if they live close to sea level. It's especially noticeable when running uphill. If a runner experiences headaches, nausea, dizziness, loss of appetite—all symptoms of acute mountain sickness—he or she should descend at once. Symptoms usually will then disappear.

Getting Lost

Most of the routes in this book are on well-established trails. A few, however, do use less-traveled trails as connections or are in areas with so many trails and dirt roads that it's easy to miss a turn or take the wrong one. Carry a map when running in areas with which you're unfamiliar. When passing trail junctions or other landmarks on out-and-back, or lollipop, routes, where you'll be returning to the same place, take a look around so that you'll know you're running the correct way on your return.

When in doubt, don't just forge ahead in the hopes that you'll find the right way or that someone might find you. Turn around, retrace your steps, and return again another day to take another shot at the route. If you don't mind the extra weight, take a cell phone along (but be aware that universal reception is not a given).

Certain mountain routes are likely to require short snow crossings, especially if run in early summer. Follow cairns or boot trails, but only if conditions are clear enough that you can see ahead to where the trail continues on land. If you can't, don't proceed. Also, don't continue if the snow is at all icy. Whole books are written about, and courses offered on, snow travel, so if you plan on doing a lot of this, do more research.

Think about the consequences of your actions and how you'd get out if you were to suffer an injury that would make continuing impossible. And of course, always let someone know where you're going ahead of time.

Night Running

During the fall and winter when the Northwest sun sets early, many trail runners don mountaineering headlights or carry flashlights to light their way on the trails at night. Nighttime trail running is a truly surreal experience, but given its high potential for falls as well as ankle and knee twists, it is also one that requires extra care. For safety's sake, never run trails alone at night, and because you can't see nearly as well, slow down. Carry a spare bulb and batteries. If running in a group, be sure to stop every so often to make sure everyone is accounted for. Lastly, dress warmly for night running, which is likely to be colder than running during the day.

Etiquette/Ethics

To protect those places that trail runners run, not only for us but for all users, stay on established trails, don't cut switchbacks, and stay off sensitive areas. Leave no trace, pack out your trash, and respect other trail users. When approaching hikers from behind, announce yourself in advance—an "On your left/right" works well—and let them know how many more are with you. Uphill runners yield to downhill runners and all runners yield to hikers and backpackers.

On multi-use trails, cyclists yield to runners/hikers, who yield to equestrians. When approaching horses, pass by on the uphill side of the trail and try not to startle the animal. Talk quietly to the horse so that it knows where you are. And because you're having such a great time using Washington's trails, volunteer your services by lending a hand on a trail-building or repair project.

Cougars and Bears

Though rare, encounters between trail runners and these large critters do occur from time to time. This is yet another reason it's a good idea not to run alone, especially in more primitive or isolated areas. If you do encounter a bear or cougar, heed the following advice from the Department of Fish and Wildlife.

Bear

Stop running and give the bear plenty of room to get away. Avoid eye contact but speak softly to the bear while backing away from it. Try not to show fear and don't turn your back on a bear. If you can't get away from it, clap your hands or yell in an effort to scare it away. If the bear becomes aggressive, fight back using anything at your disposal. Should the attack continue, curl up in a ball or lie down on your stomach and play dead.

Cougar

Stop running, and don't take your eyes off the cougar. Make yourself appear big by raising your arms above your head and opening your jacket if you're wearing one. Also wave a stick above your head. If the cougar approaches, yell and throw rocks, sticks, anything you can get your hands on. In the event of an attack, fight back aggressively.

Personally, when I'm running by myself in potential bear or cougar territory, I like carrying a stick about 18 inches long that I can wave above my head in the event of an encounter. (I haven't had to use it yet.) It's also great for pushing brush out of the way on especially overgrown trails and clearing spider webs on early morning runs.

About This Book

Trail Running Guide to Western Washington is for runners of all levels. Beginners will find a number of routes that offer wide, mostly level trails that are under 4 miles. Intermediate trail runners and beginners who want to bump up to the next level will find numerous routes of up to about 10 to 12 miles that offer hills, thrills, and the potential for spills, and that gain 1,000 to 3,000 feet in elevation. And experienced, hard-core, and ultra runners will be challenged by routes that feature heavy mileage and/or more than 3,500 feet of climbing.

In addition, this book offers many alternative routes, so that runners can shorten or lengthen the featured route. This is especially useful for groups or couples of varying levels who want to run from the same trailhead. Each route description also includes information on the nearest food, camping, and accommodations.

All of the routes are easy to get to and most are within one hour of one of Puget Sound's major cities—Bellingham, Everett, Seattle, Tacoma, and Olympia. Most of the book's routes can be run year-round, though about fifteen featured or alternative routes are in the Cascade or Olympic mountains and are runnable only part of the year.

In choosing which trails to include, I considered what percentage of the route can be run, the opportunities for great views and adventure, variety, terrain, trail conditions, and other trail users. I arranged many routes so that the strenuous climbing is done early in the run.

Trail Running Guide to Western Washington is different from a hiking guide in that it includes information vital and specific to runners. Not all hiking trails lend themselves to running, so all of the routes in this book have been selected with runners specifically in mind. I point out potential running hazards such as rocky and root-strewn sections, let runners know about particularly steep or technical stretches, and provide how-to tips on the best ways to maneuver the Northwest's winding, roller-coaster trails. There is information geared toward runners about where to find water, where the best places are to eat and drink, and how to take advantage of a route's flat and downhill sections. And of course, I highlight the views, which are in great abundance on most Western Washington trails.

That said, hikers, walkers, and other outdoor enthusiasts will likely find this book useful as well for its sheer variety and the easy accessibility of routes. After all, it's probably the only book that includes descriptions of the 2.6-mile Mercer Slough Nature Park loop in Bellevue as well as the 30-mile Loowit Trail around Mount St. Helens.

How to Use This Book

For each of the fifty featured routes, there is a detailed description, a topo-graphical map and elevation profile, and frequently, a photograph. At the beginning of each route description is a list of vital statistics and other useful information for each route. Here's an explanation of the "route at a glance" list that begins each trail write-up:

Pain 🏃

This is a measure of the route's difficulty, rated on a scale of 1 to 5, with 1 being the easiest, 5 the most challenging. Hills, how technical a trail is, dis-tance, and elevation were all taken into consideration in determining the trail's pain factor.

Gain ▲

Here you'll find the route's fun factor as determined by its opportunities for views, wilderness experience, adventure, and overall appeal.

Distance

These are estimates. Determining distances on trails is difficult as maps are not always accurate and are often at odds with trail signs. I measured some trails with a mountain bike odometer, but not all the trails in this book allow bikes.

Elevation Gain

This is the total amount (in feet) of climbing that each route requires.

Time

Once again, an estimate. I based times on distance and assumed an 8-minute mile for the fastest runners and a 15-minute mile for the slower ones. This is highly variable, since on shorter, flatter routes some people will average 6 minutes per mile, whereas on some long, steep, technical sections, others would be closer to 20-30 minutes per mile.

The Route

Here's a brief one- or two-sentence description to let runners know what they're getting into. You'll find information about the running surface, terrain (i.e., forest, beach, alpine, etc.), whether or not the route offers views and signs. **Signs** means every intersection is signed; **Some signs** means not all intersections are signed; **No signs** means you're on your own.

   A note on some words used in the descriptions. **Single track** refers to a narrow trail wide enough for one person. You won't be doing any side-by-side running on these. **Technical** refers to trails—usually single tracks and often steep ones—that are marked by rocks, roots, logs, and other obstacles.

Alternative Route

Here's where readers will find a variation on the main route that's profiled. The alternative can be either longer or shorter than the main route and usually is significantly different—i.e., much longer/shorter, more hilly/flat, more/less technical. In almost every case, the alternative route uses the same trailhead as the main route.

Runnability

This is the percentage of the route that most people should be able to *run* and not walk. In determining this percentage, I mostly took into consideration a route's steepness. Not to get too complicated, but here's how my highly complex MMcQ formula works: If I could run 80 percent of the trail, but had to walk 20, I figure the average runner will be able to run 80 percent but have to walk 20. This was based on: (1) I'm of average speed, (2) I'm not particularly fast, and (3) I'm not particularly slow.

Season

Most of the book's routes can be run year-round. For mountain routes on which trails are snow-covered most of the year, the running season is indicated.

Other Users

This lists the route's other users, such as hikers, mountain bikers, equestrians, etc.

Map

A list of useful maps pertinent to the route is provided.

Permit

If a route requires a Northwest Forest Pass, you'll find that information here.

Route Descriptions

After the "route at a glance" list of vital stats, there is a description of each route, with the following sections:

Warm-up

This offers more details and background on the route—what makes this route unique or special, what kinds of views runners can expect, what its calling card is. It's essentially what you would tell your friends after running a particular route.

Approach

Here's where you'll find driving directions to the trailhead from the nearest major highway. The trailhead elevation is also included.

Go

As the heading implies, this is where you actually start running. Along with route directions, you'll find what to look out for and look forward to—killer views, killer uphills, fun-as-heck downhills, easy-to-miss turnoffs, and so forth. Everything you need to know to successfully and enjoyably run the route is here. Distances to selected intersections and landmarks along the way are also included.

Nearest Support

This is kind of the before and after information for each route. You'll find out whether or not the trailhead has rest rooms, water, and telephones, as well as the closest food and accommodations. Important phone numbers and Web sites are also included.

Route Maps

A map and elevation profile accompany every route description. These show general topography, elevation gain and loss, start/end points, direction of travel, and major land features and destinations. Keep in mind that these maps are basically illustrative and are not a replacement for actual USGS, USFS, or Green Trails maps.

Map Legend

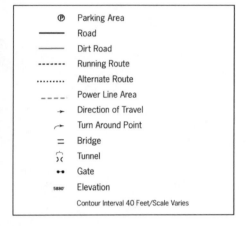

1

BELLINGHAM / MOUNT VERNON

North Lake Whatcom

PAIN 🏃

GAIN ▲ ▲ ▲

Distance	6.2 miles out and back
Elevation gain	50 feet
Time	45 minutes to 1.25 hours
The route	Mostly wide, flat railroad grade and trail along picturesque lake. Views. No signs.
Runnability	100 percent
Season	Year-round
Other users	Hikers, bikers
Map	USGS Lake Whatcom (7.5' series)

Warm-up

On those hot summer days, this old railroad bed is just about the perfect running route. Why? It's shaded almost the entire way, has no hills on which to battle gravity, and, last but best, it's bordered by Lake Whatcom. Countless opportunities to take the Nestea plunge are just 10 feet away during most of

Cruising along North Lake Whatcom trail

the entire route. Check out the scenic waterfall and huge rock bluff too. Half-mile markers denote the trail.

Approach

From Interstate 5, take exit 253 in Bellingham. Head south on King Street and then left just ahead on Lakeway Boulevard. Drive east on Lakeway for 1.7 miles to Electric Avenue. Turn left and after 1.2 miles, at a three-way intersection, the

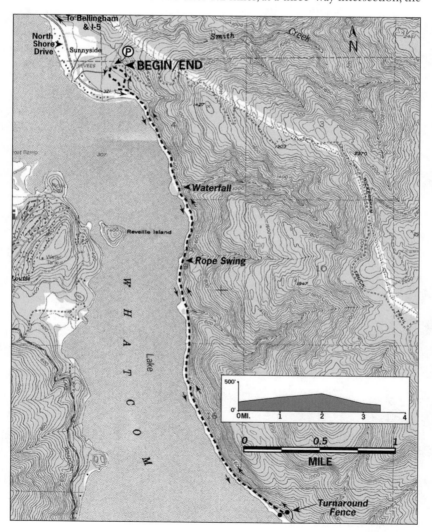

road becomes North Shore Drive. Continue on North Shore for 8.3 miles. At a North Lake Whatcom Trailhead sign, turn left. The trailhead parking lot is a half-mile farther on the left. Elevation: 360 feet.

Go

From the parking lot, follow the wide gravel and dirt trail—with a short stretch of boardwalk thrown in—through forest for about 0.25 mile. At the T-intersection with the railroad grade trail, run left. No turns are required for the next 3 miles so put your running mechanism on autopilot. Before you do, however, take note of the trail that leads left and back into the woods from whence you've just come. For variety's sake, that's the way you'll return to the parking lot.

At 1.0 mile let out an ooh and an aah for the waterfall a-plungin' and a-splashin' about 50 yards up and to the left. About 0.25 mile ahead, an impressive 100-plus-foot rock wall begins poking through the trees. At 1.5 miles, an open area with a rope hanging from a tree invites you to cut your run short to take a flying leap. Save it for the way back, or engage in your own multi-sport challenge: trail running, rope swinging/diving, and rock skipping.

At 3.1 miles the trail ends abruptly at a no-nonsense NO TRESPASSING–signed fence. Turn around and return the way you came, taking a swing on the rope and the variety's-sake trail back to the parking lot.

Nearest Support

A portable toilet is the only trailhead support. Whatcom County Parks and Recreation information, 360/733-2900, or www.co.whatcom.wa.us/parks/trails/lkwhatc/lkwhatc.htm. Bellingham, which offers plentiful foodstuffs, drinkstuffs, and accommodations, is about 8 miles away off Lakeway Boulevard.

2 Lookout Mountain Towers

PAIN 🏃🏃

GAIN ▲▲▲

Distance	6 miles out and back
Elevation gain	1,250 feet
Time	50 minutes to 1.5 hours
The route	Steadily climbing logging road. Some pavement. Views. No signs.
Runnability	100 percent
Season	Year-round
Other users	Bikers, hikers, motorcyclists, ATV users, equestrians
Maps	Galbraith (Local Knowledge Trail Map); USGS Bellingham South (7.5' series)

Warm-up

Lookout Mountain, also known as Galbraith Mountain, is a Department of Natural Resources/private property mix that's a playground for off-road enthusiasts of every stripe. Because there are so many trails here, almost none of them signed, what follows is a get-acquainted, out-and-back on a hard-to-get-lost logging road.

Approach

From Interstate 5, take exit 246 and head northwest on Samish Way. Drive 1.4 miles to an unmarked parking lot on the left at the crest of a hill. Elevation: 900 feet.

Go

From the parking lot, take a right on Samish Way and run on pavement for about 50 yards to Galbraith Lane, also paved. Turn left. At **0.3** mile, take the first right. Ignore the NO TRESPASSING signs that seem to be mounted everywhere. (Don't worry, you're not doing anything illegal.) Just ahead, the road forks into two dirt roads. Take the left fork, rounding a gate as you do. (The countless tire tracks and footprints will assure you that you're not the first to do this.)

Almost immediately, the road starts climbing. This Lookout Mountain is an interesting place. Parts have a post-nuclear war/Mad Max feel and at times

On the road to Lookout Mountain Towers

you think that the reason it's called Lookout Mountain is because you spend half your time having to look out for motorcyclists, ATV hot rods, and mountain bikers. Other parts boast forest that's so dense it blocks out the sun. What makes it work are the eagle's-eye views, some of the best around, of Bellingham, the San Juan and Gulf Islands, and Canada's Coast Mountains.

At 1.1 miles, round a bend and catch the first views of your goal: three telecommunication towers that look like giant lunar modules from the Apollo space program. Run backward for a few steps and ooh and aah over the views west toward Bellingham Bay and the San Juans, which improve with each foot of elevation gained.

At 1.4 miles, run right at what locals call Blue Rock Junction—the rock that's been spray painted blue is the giveaway—following an orange arrow mounted on a telephone pole. Bear right at another fork at 2.0 miles, once again following a helpful orange arrow. The towers loom large at this point.

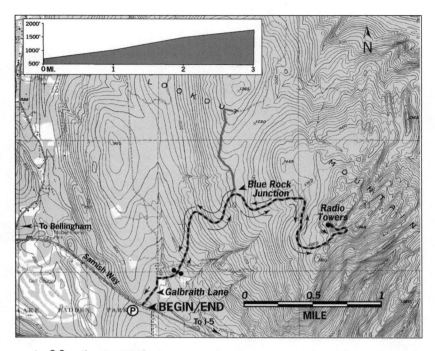

At **2.3** miles (1,470 feet), a great view opens up to the right on a mostly level stretch of trail. Drink up for the final push while admiring the stunning island, mountain, water, and city views. In the distance, gunshots can be heard but don't be alarmed. The Plantation Rifle, Pistol, and Trap Range is located on the south flank of Lookout Mountain. From this distance, the shots sound like surfacing whales breathing through their blowholes. Pretend that's what it is.

About 200 yards ahead, bear to the left at a fork and resume climbing. Enter a small, but thick stand of trees at **2.6** miles, nodding at a tower on your right as you pass. Take a left at another fork a few hundred yards ahead and suck it up for the final winding 0.25-mile push to the top. At **3.0** miles, you're there, at the foot of two giant steel radio towers. Unfortunately, trees allow only obscured views south and west. That's okay. You can jam to the views on the cruise down, which is a blast. Return the way you came.

Nearest Support

The Samish Way parking lot offers no water and only a portable toilet. Closest eats, drinks, and sleeps are about 4 miles from the trailhead on Bellingham's Samish Way strip.

3 Lookout Mountain Intestine

PAIN 🏃🏃

GAIN ▲▲▲

Distance	5.4-mile lollipop loop
Elevation gain	900 feet
Time	45 minutes to 1.25 hours
The route	Everything from open logging road to technical single track through dense forest. Views. No signs.
Alternative route	9.2-mile route connecting Lookout Towers and Lookout Intestine
Runnability	100 percent
Season	Year-round
Other users	Bikers, hikers, motorcyclists, ATV users, equestrians
Maps	Galbraith (Local Knowledge Trail Map); USGS Bellingham South (7.5' series)

Warm-up

This route explores the lower reaches of Lookout Mountain's northwest flank. Along with some long straightaways, you'll zig and zag through forest so dense the sun disappears on the brightest days. *Caution:* This trail, like many on Lookout Mountain (also known as Galbraith Mountain), is beloved by mountain bikers and motorcyclists also.

Approach

From Interstate 5, take exit 246 and head northwest on Samish Way. Drive 1.4 miles to an unmarked parking lot on the left at the crest of a hill. Elevation: 900 feet.

Go

From the parking lot, take a right on Samish Way and run on pavement for about 50 yards to paved Galbraith Lane. Take a left. At **0.3** mile, continue straight at T-intersection. The pavement ends just ahead, and not far after that you come to a fork and two gated dirt roads. Take the one on the right, pass beyond the gate, and begin a gradual climb.

At **0.8** mile bear left at a four-way trail-and-dirt-road intersection and begin a long, wide straightaway that feels like it's cutting through the middle

Along the flank of Lookout Mountain

of two forests. Continue climbing gradually, letting your curiosity run wild about the several trails leading into the dark woods on both sides of the road. Those are for another day, my friend, when you are more familiar with this land they call Galbraith.

At **1.8** miles, after cresting a hill and taking in some Bellingham and Canadian peak views, turn right up an obvious logging road that enters a former clear-cut area. Begin a fairly steep 0.25-mile climb. After rounding a bend, the hill drops the "fairly" part and is just plain steep. Once at the top, take a right at the second unmarked trail.

Follow as the trail winds and descends for a few hundred yards to an intersection at the edge of a forest. A sign nailed to a tree declares this the "Family Fun Center." (The Family Fun Center is serious mountain-bike territory, so the trails are technical, tend toward the muddy, and are often populated by those on two wheels.) Take a left, enter the woods, and immediately cross a wood bridge. Just across, take a right at the first intersection and, bypassing a couple of lefts, continue as the trail makes a leisurely bend to the left around a corner.

Follow as the trail starts climbing and crosses a dirt road. At **2.6** miles, the

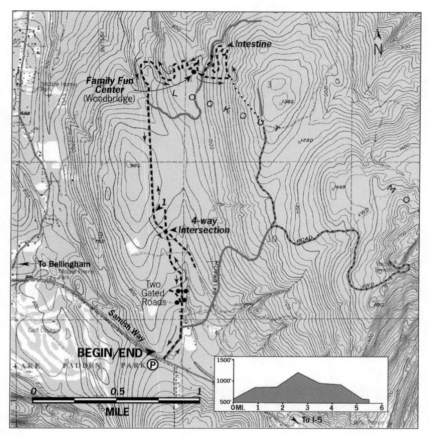

trail bends to the left and continues along the back edge of the forest. A few hundred yards ahead at a four-way intersection, take a left and reenter the woods. The forest here is deep, dense, and dark. Compounding that is the fact that the trail weaves and winds quickly through these trees, thus its name: the Intestine. (Yes, it does take a lot of guts to run the Intestine.) Take a moment for your eyes to adjust and to get your footing, then let 'er rip. Over the next 0.5 mile, the Intestine switchbacks a couple of times, then comes to a T. Take a left and then another quick left onto a dirt road.

After descending slightly for about 300 yards, take a right on the trail that you ascended to get to the Intestine. (You ran straight through this intersection, not long ago.) At this point, retrace your steps out of the Family Fun Center. Return the way you came.

Alternate Route

This 9.2-mile alternate route combines Lookout Towers and Lookout Intestine. Run the Lookout Mountain Intestine route, but just before entering the Intestine, take a right instead of a left. Run uphill for about 0.25 mile to a dirt road. Continue straight through to an intersection with another dirt road. Take a right and follow this mostly level road for a little more than 0.5 mile to an intersection with another dirt road. This is Blue Rock Junction. From here, follow directions given for Run #2, Lookout Mountain Towers. Return the way you came.

Nearest Support

The Samish Way parking lot offers no water and only a portable toilet. Closest eats, drinks, and sleeps are about 4 miles from the trailhead on Bellingham's Samish Way strip.

4 Lake Padden

PAIN

GAIN ▲ ▲

Distance	2.6-mile loop
Elevation gain	70 feet
Time	20 to 40 minutes
The route	Wide dirt trail around a lake. Minor rolling hills through forest. No signs.
Alternate route	6-mile route that's hilly and fairly technical in spots
Runnability	100 percent
Season	Year-round
Other users	Bikers, hikers, equestrians
Maps	Lake Padden (Local Knowledge Trail Map); USGS Bellingham South (7.5' series)

Warm-up

(*Caution:* Hackneyed phraseology ahead!) Lake Padden offers something for trail runners of all levels. (There.) Beginners can run the 2.6-mile lake loop to get a sense of what trail running is about. Those in a speedwork mood can uti-

The wide trail around Lake Padden

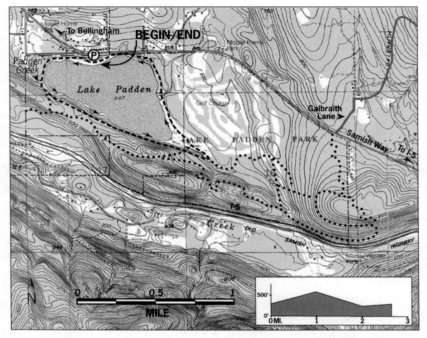

lize the posts marking quarter-mile intervals along the trail. Technical trail rats can head off on the myriad trails leading from the lake's south and east sides.

Approach

From Interstate 5 just south of Bellingham, take exit 246. Head northwest on Samish Way for about 3 miles to the Lake Padden Park West Entrance. (It's about 0.4 mile past the east entrance.) Park here. Elevation: 450 feet.

Go

From the parking lot, head toward the lake and run right on the obvious, wide trail. Stay on this trail all the way around, keeping the lake on your left side and ignoring the many trails that beckon to the right. At **0.3** mile as you enter a heavily wooded area, climb a short hill just after crossing a bridge over Padden Creek. After about a 150-yard climb, follow the main trail as it bears to the left and roller coasters gently over the next 1.3 miles. At **1.6** miles, the trail emerges from the woods near some softball fields. From here it's a flat mile back to the parking lot.

Alternate Route

Just after cresting that first 150-yard hill, continue straight and keep climbing for about 300 yards. Take a left at a four-way intersection. From here, run wherever you want over trails that are hilly and at times fairly technical. Trails seem to head off in all directions, so let your trail-running soul improvise. With Lake Padden and Lake Padden Golf Course to the north, and I-5 to the south, it's almost impossible to get lost. *Caution:* The only thing that keeps this area from being a true trail-runner's Mecca is its popularity with mountain bikers and equestrians.

Nearest Support

In spring and summer, Lake Padden Park offers rest rooms and water, the rest of the year just portable toilets. Bellingham Parks and Recreation, 360/676-6985 or www.cob.org/cobweb/parks/pages/facilities.html. Closest eats, drinks, and sleeps are about 2 miles away on Bellingham's Samish Way strip.

5 Hemlock Trail/Raptor Ridge

PAIN 🏃🏃🏃

GAIN ▲▲▲

Distance	9.4 miles out and back
Elevation gain	1,500 feet
Time	1.25 to 2.25 hours
The route	Single track, old logging road, and some pavement. Dense forest opening to sweeping views. Signed.
Runnability	95 percent
Season	Year-round
Other users	Bikers, hikers, equestrians
Map	Chuckanut (Local Knowledge Trail Map)

Warm-up

This route is a great way to familiarize yourself with some of the newer trails on Chuckanut Mountain's north flank. The recently opened 4-mile Hemlock Trail connects the popular Lost Lake Trail with the Pine and Cedar Lakes Trail. The 0.3-mile Raptor Ridge Trail is a magical offshoot of the Hemlock and thrusts runners into deep forest before revealing an impressive vista.

Rock-hopping on Raptor Ridge

Approach

From Interstate 5, take exit 250 and head west on Old Fairhaven Parkway. Park in the Interurban Trail Rotary Trailhead parking lot 0.9 mile ahead on the left. Elevation: 100 feet.

Go

Pick up the wide gravel trail and after a quick down and up, run left on the sidewalk for about a hundred yards. (Head for the brown and yellow trail posts.) Cross 20th Street and regain the wide, gravel Interurban Trail. After crossing another residential street, follow the flat route as it bends to the right and heads south.

At **1.1** miles, run left at a fork and drop down before crossing Old Samish Highway. Once across, descend into a verdant, overgrown canyon and run the mini–roller coaster that parallels Chuckanut Creek. After a few hundred yards, cross the creek on a wood bridge and climb a short series of switchbacks. At **1.6** miles, turn left following the sign for Lost Lake.

The trail climbs quickly, steeply, and, depending on what time of year it is, muddily. Soon enough the trail levels out and eventually switchbacks to the right up a wide shoulder and connects with an old logging road. Run left.

Just ahead, at **2.3** miles, a signed intersection informs you that Raptor Ridge is 2.3 miles away and that you are now on the Hemlock Trail. Continue straight ahead. After about 0.3 mile, begin climbing fairly steadily. At **3.4** miles, at an intersection with the Salal Trail, continue straight, following the sign for Raptor Ridge.

The trail narrows down to single track. About 0.25 mile ahead, look to the left on clear days for views of Mount Baker peaking through the alders. The trail climbs a bit, becomes more technical, and eventually enters an older section of forest. About 100 yards in run right, following the sign for Raptor Ridge.

Almost immediately, you enter a deep, dark, cavelike section of forest that's like a good-time obstacle course with its wood bridge, huge boulders, and stone and wood steps. Watch your noggin: Overhanging rocks make the notion of trail-running helmets seem like a good one. The forest canopy is so dense on this 0.3-mile stretch of trail that the air feels about 15 degrees cooler than it does just outside.

Eventually, the trail opens up to a 180-degree awe-inspiring vista high atop a rock cliff. You'll find plenty of room and rock on which to take a load off, refuel, and stare silently at the vast open space ahead of you. Be careful, though. It's a long drop. Also, try not to be too intrusive. The trail has earned

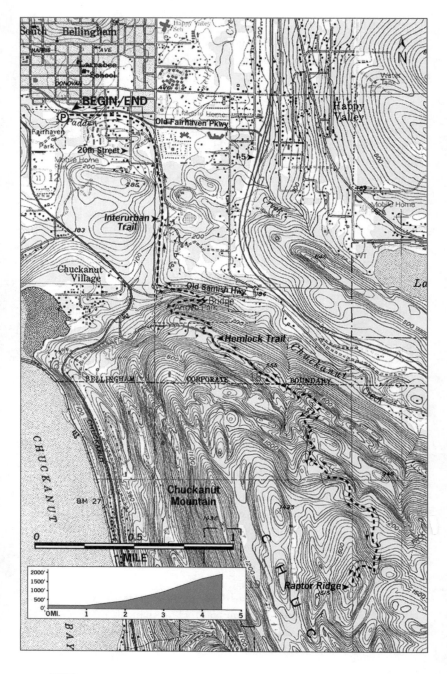

its name because various hawks nest in the area and eagles are often spotted flying overhead. Eat, drink, then return the way you came.

Nearest Support

The Interurban Trail Rotary trailhead offers only a portable toilet. For general information, contact Bellingham Parks and Recreation, 360/676-6985. Bellingham's Fairhaven district is a little more than a mile from the trailhead and is a fine source of food, drink, and places to stay.

6 Chuckanut Ridge-Lost Lake Loop

PAIN 🏃🏃🏃

GAIN ▲▲▲

Distance	8.9-mile loop
Elevation gain	1,850 feet
Time	1.25 to 2.25 hours
The route	Technical single track and old logging road. Ups and downs through forests and along ridges. Views. Some signs.
Alternate route	4.7-mile loop
Runnability	90 percent; 100 percent for alternate route
Season	Year-round
Other users	Bikers, hikers, equestrians
Maps	Chuckanut (Local Knowledge Trail Map); USGS Bellingham South (7.5' series)

Warm-up

This route—which makes up the middle portion of the Chuckanut Mountain 50K Race—connects two popular trails, Chuckanut Ridge and Lost Lake, and adds a third, Little Chinscraper. The result is a run that offers the best and most

Runners in the 2000 Chuckanut 50K

that Chuckanut Mountain has to offer: the best views, the most technical trail, the best chance to spot wildlife, the most climbing, the best excuse to walk, and in many trail runners' opinions, the most fun.

Approach

From Interstate 5, take exit 231 in Burlington. Drive north on Highway 11 (Chuckanut Drive) to milepost 16. Immediately after the milepost, take a right on Hiline Road, which soon becomes a dirt road named Cleator Road. Follow Cleator for about 3.6 miles—climbing about 1,500 feet—almost to the end. Park at a switchback near the sign for Lost Lake Overlook, or about 100 yards farther at the Cyrus Gates Overlook parking lot. Elevation: 1,740 feet.

Go

At the Lost Lake Overlook sign, enter the thick woods via the obvious Chuckanut Ridge Trail. Over the next 3 miles, the easy-to-follow, rock- and root-studded single track snakes along Chuckanut Mountain's spine, offering stunning views of Mount Baker and her Cascade siblings. Enjoy, but be careful. The trail runs along the top of a 200-foot sandstone cliff, and some stretches are perilously close the edge.

Continue north enjoying the trail's mini ups and downs. You'll feel like you're dancing as you slalom through massive trees and giant, smooth boulders that resemble the backs of whales. At **2.3** miles ignore a trail leading to the left. About 0.5 mile ahead, descend sharply down some large, flat, and usually slippery boulder faces. When the trail levels out a bit at **3.0** miles, turn right on Banana Peel Way, an easy-to-miss, unsigned spur. Look for an unusually bent tree trunk, about 5 feet tall, that resembles a backward question mark. (If you end up in a residential area, you've gone about 0.25 mile too far.) Drop quickly and to the right across a steep side slope for a few hundred yards. Just ahead, cross a creek and arrive at Lost Lake Trail. Run right. (*Note:* During rainy season, Banana Peel Way earns its name and will likely have you reaching for limbs and roots to help you stay upright.)

Head south along Lost Lake Trail, an overgrown dirt road, for about 2 miles, encountering a mix of steep climbs and level stretches. Marvel at the massive sandstone face to your right and mini-waterfalls splashing down it. In winter and spring, it might help if you pretend not to notice that the road gradually degenerates into a narrow tube of muck and mire.

At **5.3** miles, arrive at a T and a sign pointing straight ahead to Lost Lake and right to Fragrance Lake Road. Consider taking a quarter-mile side trip

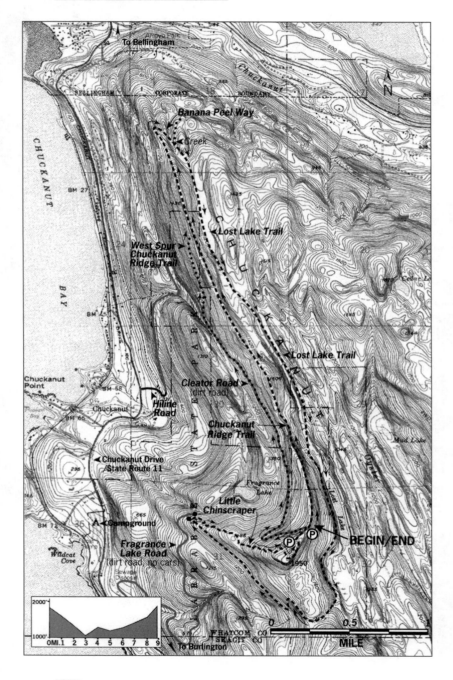

down to the lake. Lost Lake is a great place to replenish your reserves with some food and drink—and to contemplate (i.e., dread) the upcoming Little Chinscraper. If you're eager to take on the Chinscraper (and take one on the chin, so to speak) turn right and, after a flat stretch, climb steadily for about 1.2 miles to a saddle and another T.

Bear right, following the sign for Lost Lake Trailhead, and let 'er rip. Over the next 1.2 miles, the trail, once again an overgrown dirt road, drops almost 500 feet. You'll think you're invincible. That'll change.

At **7.7** miles, at a GATE AHEAD sign, find an obscure trail leading to the right and to a serious ascent. Little Chinscraper is what the trail is called; big pain is what it causes. In 0.9 mile this ridiculously steep, rock- and root-strewn connector climbs almost 850 feet. So do what most trail runners do here: walk. Along the way, admire the beakwork of pileated woodpeckers who've bored football-sized holes in seemingly every snag along the way. Catch views of Puget Sound from time to time as they pop up through the trees. Truth be told, it's quite a pleasant forest hike, albeit a steep one.

At the top, catch your breath and pat yourself on the back—you've made it to 1,950 feet, the highest point on Chuckanut Mountain! The trail continues, descending about 100 yards, then opens out into the Cyrus Gates Overlook parking lot. Your starting point at the Lost Lake Overlook sign is a few hundred yards down the road to the right.

Alternate Route

For a shorter, non-mud, non-Chinscraper loop of 4.7 miles, take a left off the Chuckanut Ridge Trail at **2.3** miles onto the unsigned, but easy-to-follow West Spur Chuckanut Ridge Trail (about 0.7 mile before the Banana Peel). The West Spur drops quickly, then levels out as it leads 0.9 mile back to Cleator Road. Take a left on Cleator and run the remaining 1.5 mostly uphill miles back to where you parked.

Nearest Support

Larrabee State Park, about 5 miles south of the trailhead, offers rest rooms, water, telephones, and camping. Information, 360/676-2093 or www.parks.wa. gov/larrabee.htm. For eats, drinks, and sleeps, Belling~~~~ north of the trailhead off Chuckanut Drive.

7 Blanchard Mountain Loop

PAIN 🏃🏃🏃

GAIN ▲ ▲ ▲

Distance	6-mile loop
Elevation gain	1,200 feet
Time	50 minutes to 1.5 hours
The route	Technical and smooth single track. One hellish Stairmaster-type climb. Views. Signs, but somewhat confusing.
Runnability	90 percent
Season	Year-round
Other users	Bikers, hikers, equestrians
Maps	Blanchard (Local Knowledge Trail Map); USGS Bellingham South (7.5' series)

Warm-up

The eagle's-eye views from this route's trailhead are better than what you get on most trails. Puget Sound, Olympic Mountains, San Juan Islands, eagles, hang gliders, and more—oh my! They get better on the trail, but you have to pay for them in the form of a steep, rocky, mega-climb. The rest is fun—otherworldly lakes and marshes, giant boulders, downhills that'll have you yelling yippee!

Island views from Blanchard Mountain

Approach

Take Interstate 5 to exit 240 and head west on Samish Lake Road. After 0.4 mile, turn left onto Barrel Springs Road, following the sign for the Blanchard Hill Trail System. At **0.6** mile take a right onto B–1000, a somewhat obscure dirt road. A Blanchard Hill sign points the way. Follow this dirt road for about 1.7 miles to a three-way intersection. Turn left onto B–2000, another dirt road, and head west on an at-times rough road for 2.2 miles. Park at a somewhat vague parking lot. You'll know you're there by the views and the large orange BE PREPARED TO STOP sign that's nailed to a tree. Elevation: 1,300 feet.

Go

Find the black stencil-like PNT sign and a trail heading north just beyond it. (Part of the route you're about to run is a section of the Pacific Northwest Trail, a network of trails extending from Glacier National Park in Montana to the western tip of the Olympic Peninsula.) Loosen those quads and hamstrings with a quarter-mile jaunt down the Larry Reed Trail, dropping about 300 feet as you pass through a clearcut area.

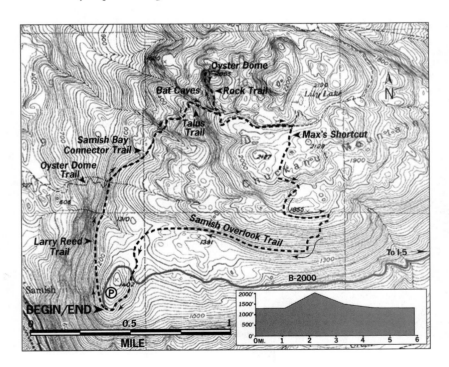

Bear right at an intersection with the Oyster Dome Trail and take a minute to familiarize yourself with the first of many somewhat-confusing-until-you-figure-out-how-to-read-them trail signs nailed to a tree. (*Hint:* If the trail name you're looking for is aligned to the left, go left; if aligned to the right, head right.) Though you haven't changed direction, you're now on the Samish Bay Connector Trail.

Traverse the side of a hill and, soon after, continue straight at another intersection. At about 1.5 miles, start what is called steep climbing. You'll gain more than 400 feet over the next 0.5 mile and feel good about it (once it's over). Take advantage of the rough trail's rocks and roots, which offer plenty to grab onto. Not far into the climb, ignore the trail to the left that leads to what is known locally as the Bat Caves. They're a jumble of boulders at the foot of a 300-foot rock wall known as the Oyster Dome. Ignore that detour because you're heading to the top of the dome.

After another 0.25 mile of the steep stuff up what is now the Talus Trail, take a left on Rock Trail, your official dome highway. After a 0.5 mile of steep, rugged trail, reach the top and ooh and aah at the island and sound views that seem to stretch to infinity. Don't get too close to the edge, as in "I wanna see what them Bat Caves look like from up here." It's a 300-foot drop and you can't see them anyway. The rest of the route is mostly downhill, so this is a great place to refuel for the rest of your loop.

Return to the intersection of the Rock and Talus Trails at 2.8 miles and take a left. In a little more than 0.5 mile, reach a marshy area and Lily Lake. Like so many mountain lakes, Lily Lake is spooky and mysterious and seems right out of the Arthurian legends. Just beyond, take a right on Max's Shortcut, which starts out fairly flat for the first 0.5 mile, then drops about 500 feet over its last mile or so. At 5.2 miles, take a right on the Samish Overlook Trail and pretty much cruise in over the last flat and downhill 0.8-mile stretch to the parking lot.

Nearest Support

Blanchard Mountain, which is Department of Natural Resources property, offers no services. Bellingham, about 12 miles north off of I-5, and Burlington, about the same distance to the south, offer plenty of food, drink, and places to stay.

8 Squires Lake/Alger Mountain

PAIN 🏃🏃

GAIN ▲ ▲ ▲

Distance	5-mile lollipop loop
Elevation gain	1,200 feet
Time	40 minutes to 1.25 hours
The route	Former roadbed and technical single track along lake and narrow ridge to minor summit. Views. Some signs.
Runnability	90 percent
Season	Year-round
Other users	Bikers, hikers, equestrians
Maps	USGS Lake Whatcom, USGS Alger (both 7.5' series)

Warm-up

Fairly new (1996), Squires Lake Park is the perfect starting point for this run to the top of 1,315-foot Alger Mountain. After a nod to said lake—favored by nine out of ten beavers surveyed—enjoy a steady mile-and-a-half climb to a 360-degree stunner of a viewpoint. Let the top down (figuratively speaking) and feel the wind in your hair on the ripping downhill cruise.

Approach

From Interstate 5, take exit 242. Head east on Nulle Road for 0.9 mile to the Squires Lake trailhead parking lot on your left. Elevation: 310 feet.

Go

Find the trail at the north end of the parking lot and immediately begin a short, steep switchbacking climb to the lake. Ogle the lake for a moment, then take a right and climb steadily up an old roadbed. At **0.5** mile, turn right into the forest at a signpost reading South Ridge Trail. Just ahead, a hard switchback to the right offers the first ridge-top running and views west to Blanchard Mountain.

Run right at a fork at **0.8** mile and continue climbing along the ridge. *Caution:* Be on high alert. Several sections of the ridge offer an exposed and deadly drop-off to the right. This is no place to let your mind wander—especially

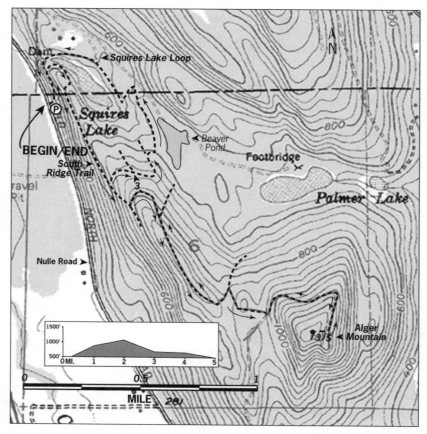

important on the way down when you'll be running faster. (Of course, then the drop-off is on your left.)

About 0.25 mile ahead, enter an open area and a T-intersection with an old logging road. Run left and continue climbing. Go straight a few hundred yards farther at another intersection, and just beyond, admire the Skagit Valley views to the south and west. After a quick dip followed by a quick ascent, your goal—Alger Mountain—appears just up ahead and to the left. Though small, its west face is nonetheless impressive.

Bear to the right at another intersection just ahead, and at **1.7** miles run left at a T-intersection with Alger Mountain's summit directly in front of you. Do the serious climbing thing—huff, puff, sweat, whatever's your pleasure—over the next 0.5 mile to the top. Check out lakes Samish and Whatcom to the north, resembling fiords with only 2,600-foot Lookout Mountain between them.

At **2.2** miles, you've made it and are immediately showered with 360-degree loveliness. On clear days, check out Mount Rainier and the Olympics to the south and west and the nearby gathering of 2,000- to 3,000-foot hills that look close enough to hit with a good spit. (They're not.)

When you've had enough, return the way you came as far as the fork you hit at the 0.7-mile mark. This time, at **3.7** miles, take a hard right onto a wide trail and drop quickly for a few hundred yards. At a T-intersection with a dirt road, run right and continue dropping. At a signed intersection, run right again following the arrow for Beaver Pond Loop. Reach Beaver Pond—which isn't really a pond so much as it is a marsh—at **4.2** miles and take a left.

Just past the Beaver Pond Loop—which isn't so much a loop as it is half of a loop—run left just before a dirt road, onto a narrow trail that drops quickly. At **4.5** miles, take a hard right following the sign for Squires Lake Loop, which is a proper loop. In a few hundred yards, reach the lily-padded lake and listen to the red-winged blackbirds tell you how much they wish you'd run elsewhere. Follow the lake, crossing a couple of bridges and running along a dirt road for another 0.25 mile or so to where you first reached the lake near the beginning of this route. Return to the parking lot the way you came.

Nearest Support

Squires Lake Park offers only a portable toilet. Whatcom County Parks and Recreation information, 360/733-2900, or www.co.whatcom.wa.us/parks/trails/squires/squires.htm. Bellingham is about 10 miles to the north off I-5, exit 252, and offers much in the way of food, drink, and accommodations.

9 Little Mountain

PAIN 🏃🏃

GAIN ▲▲▲

Distance	3.4-mile lollipop loop
Elevation gain	890 feet
Time	30 to 50 minutes
The route	Technical single track with steep ups and downs. Views. Some signs.
Runnability	95 percent
Season	Year-round
Other users	Hikers
Map	USGS Mount Vernon (7.5' series)

Warm-up

From Interstate 5 in Mount Vernon, this 934-foot bump sticks out the way a softball sticks out under the blankets on a made bed. The route is short—it's called Little Mountain after all—but plenty big on challenges, and the views from up top are king-sized. One steep stretch on the ascent makes a rope seem like a good idea; parts of the descent are double-black diamond fast.

Approach

From Interstate 5, take exit 224 and head east to a T-intersection with Cedardale Road. Turn left and drive north for about 0.25 mile to Hickox Road. Turn right. The trailhead, marked by a Darvill Trail to Little Mountain Park sign is about a mile ahead on the left. There is no parking lot and the shoulder is narrow, so park at a bend in the road 0.25 mile ahead where the shoulder is wider. Elevation: 80 feet.

Go

From where you parked, run about 0.25 mile on Hickox Road back to the trailhead. The first 0.6 mile of trail was built and is maintained by Dr. Fred Darvill, on whose property it lies. Thanks, doc! Take a moment to read the typewritten directions tacked to a tree. No bikes, horses, hunting, or smoking allowed. If you're interested in helping the good doctor maintain the trail, you're more than welcome.

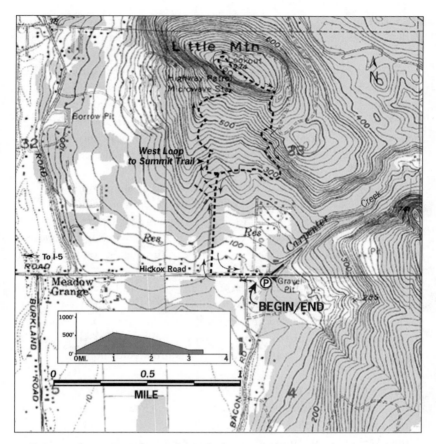

Start up the narrow, forested—and given to being somewhat overgrown—stone and wood plank path, climbing gradually at first. At **0.6** mile (from where you parked), bear to the right at an unmarked fork. A few hundred yards ahead, do the same thing, this time at a sign warning you that to go left is to enter private property.

At **0.9** mile, take a left at a T-intersection and sign pointing you to the West Loop to Little Summit Trail. Remember this spot, you'll be returning here. "Recommended for experienced strong hikers only," say the typed West Loop directions. That means us. The next 0.7 mile climbs 600 feet with a couple of vertical-tending stretches that offer the sensation of an exposed rock climb. Almost. Watch your steps, especially in wet weather.

At **1.6** miles, with the bulk of the gravity battle behind you, take a right at a Y-intersection and continue up, but not for long. Reach the roof of Little

Mountain in another 0.1 mile and take in the big-time views. Glaciated peaks, evergreen islands, bays, inlets, narrows, straits, flats, farmland, freeway— all present and fighting for attention.

Sip some water, then scamper to the far side of the gated communications towers. Find a sign reading NO BIKES and run down the major trail just to the right. (*Note*: Over this next stretch, a multitude of trails head off in seemingly all directions. Stay on the most prominent one that follows a somewhat rocky ridge down. Then again, Little Mountain *is* little. If you take the wrong trail, just find one that takes you to the hill's south side and you'll eventually be on the right track.)

After about 0.25 mile, bear right at a fork and descend even more quickly than you have been. At **2.2** miles, continue straight through a four-way inter-section following another NO BIKES sign. (That's quite the theme here on Lit-tle Mountain.) For the next 0.3 mile or so, the steep, winding descent feels like a double black-diamond ski run, so don't be surprised if you find yourself involuntarily yelling "Yee-haw!"

At **2.5** miles, not long after bearing right where the Taylor Trail beckons you left, return to the spot where you earlier took a left on the West Loop to Little Summit Trail. Turn left and return the way you came or—because the up and down to and from the summit is only 1.6 miles and the views from up top are so darn good—do another loop. And another. And another.

Nearest Support

Little Mountain offers no trailhead support. Mount Vernon Parks and Recre-ation information, 360/336-6215. Little Mountain is less than a mile from Mount Vernon, which provides plenty of opportunities for food, drink, and accommodations.

10 | Heart Lake–Mount Erie Loop

PAIN 🏃🏃🏃

GAIN ▲▲▲

Distance	6.3-mile loop
Elevation gain	1,550 feet
Time	50 minutes to 1.5 hours
The route	Wide trail and technical single track with big-time steeps. Views. Well-signed.
Runnability	90 percent
Season	Year-round
Other users	Hikers, mountain bikers, motorcyclists, equestrians
Map	Anacortes Community Forest Lands Trail Guide

Warm-up

Heart Lake and Mount Erie are pure magic! The lakeside part of this run offers a slalom-like joyride through a forest of massive firs and cedars. Steep Mount Erie boasts a high scream-for-mommy quotient, with a surprise: Sugarloaf's is even higher. Big payoffs in the views department too—Olympic Mountains, San Juan Islands, Cascades, and more.

Mount Erie views

Approach

Take Interstate 5, exit 230, and head west on Highway 20 for about 11.5 miles to where Highway 20 divides. Turn left, following Highway 20 toward Whidbey Island. At 1.8 miles, turn right onto Campbell Lake Road and after 1.6 more miles, turn right onto Heart Lake Road. Heart Lake State Park is about 2 miles ahead on your left. Elevation: 340 feet.

Go

Find the signed trailhead for Trail 210. Follow the trail into the forest and after about 0.3 mile, bear left at a T-intersection, following the sign for Trail 23. About 0.25 mile farther, bear to the left at an intersection with Trail 224. Though the winding, technical trail always stays within a few hundred yards of the lakeshore, you do lose sight of the lake from time to time due to the denseness of the forest. At these points, various mini-trails head left to the lake's shore. Ignore these but give props to the massive fir trees, especially along the lake's south shore.

At 1.8 miles, after a short, steep stretch, emerge on an old dirt road and run left. Reach Heart Lake Road about 0.25 mile farther and, after looking up and down like good little trail running boys and girls, cross. At the pullout area/entrance for Mount Erie Road, bear to the left for about 50 yards to the Sugarloaf Trail sign and trailhead. This is Trail 215, and though a big cedar just to the left sports a Trail 215 sign with a smaller trail next to it, disregard it. *Take the trail that starts right next to the Sugarloaf sign.* (A 215 sign just up the trail will put whatever doubts you have to rest.)

Forested 215 starts out flat enough. Up to this point, the route has gained only 140 feet, so you might think that this is one of the book's more tame routes. Think again. After about 150 yards, just after passing an unsigned trail to the left, 215 makes a sharp bend to the right and takes a turn for the steep. Over the next 0.7 mile, climb almost 700 feet, bearing to the right at the signed 225–215 intersection along the way. Shortly after some views begin to open up to the right, take the second left at an Anacortes Community Forest Lands (ACFL) sign. This sign is like the numbered trail signs you've seen along the way, except that this one doesn't have a number. It's Trail 228. Trust me.

Take a left and after a short, switchbacking climb, take a right at a T-intersection, following the 239 Loop sign. You're at the top of Sugarloaf here, so take a few minutes to enjoy the views that are offered—about 270 degrees worth of magic. Mount Erie, next on your list, is directly ahead—and above—

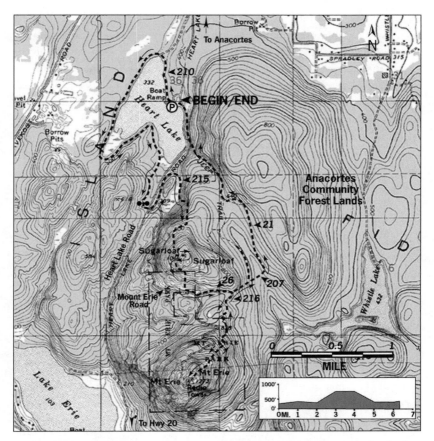

to the south. Notice how it seems you have to head down quite a bit before you resume climbing. Interesting.

Head back down 228 and take a left this time on 215. Descend sharply almost immediately. Just ahead, at an unmarked intersection, take a left and continue dropping for a few hundred yards, finally reaching Mount Erie Road at about **3.1** miles.

Take a left and run the road for about 150 yards and take a left back into the woods at the sign for a bunch of trails, including Mount Erie Summit Trail. Run wide, flat Trail 26 for about 0.25 mile to an intersection with Trail 207. Go straight, following the sign for Mount Erie, but remember this inter-section because you'll be back. This is Trail 216, which almost immediately narrows down to single track, and then to a technical one at that. Rocks, roots, downed logs, mud if you're in the mood (or even if you're not)—they're all here. So is that other thing—what's it called? Oh yeah: serious elevation gain. You'll climb more than 500 feet over the 0.7-mile jaunt to the summit. Some stretches are so steep, it's best to use your hands to help you climb up over particularly rocky, rooty sections. Makeshift ladders have been installed at one point to help hikers and runners on the way to the top. *Note:* At several points the trail diverges. Don't worry: The two branches will meet up just ahead. For comfort's sake, take the one that appears more well traveled.

At **3.8** miles, reach Mount Erie's summit (1,273 feet). Views are of the bird's-eye variety, especially to the southwest where it feels you're looking straight down onto Lake Erie.

As evil as it sounds, I recommend running the road for the beginning of the descent. Yes, running on pavement is no walk on the trails, but running down the last stretch of Mount Erie Trail is an invitation for ankle, knee, and other body part bust-up. A little more than 0.25 mile down the road, at the elbow of a sharp curve to the left, is an entrance on the right to the trail you just climbed. Duck back into the forest, take a left on the trail, and continue descending. It's fast and technical, so be careful.

At the Trail 207 intersection that you passed earlier, run right and continue dropping rapidly. Ignore Trail 230, which leads to the left after about 0.25 mile, but just ahead, after a sharp ascent, take a left at a T-intersection with Trail 21. It's wide, not too rocky, and starts climbing almost immediately, though not in the Sugarloaf–Erie vein. Continue straight for almost a mile ignoring a couple of unsigned trails on either side. At about **5.7** miles, bear right at a major fork with an unsigned trail. (The left drops quickly, the right stays level.) From here it's just a bit more than a 0.5-mile easy downhill jaunt back to Heart Lake Road and the park just across the road.

Nearest Support

Heart Lake State Park offers no water and only a pit toilet. Anacortes Community Forest Lands information, 360/293-1918. Closest food, drink, and places to stay are on Commercial Avenue in Anacortes, about 2 miles north of Heart Lake.

11

Whistle Lake

PAIN 🏃🏃

GAIN ▲ ▲ ▲

Distance	6.2-mile lollipop loop
Elevation gain	940 feet
Time	1 to 1.5 hours
The route	Technical single track and wide trail through forest and wetland. Well-signed. Views.
Alternate routes	Two of varying lengths and difficulties
Runnability	100 percent
Season	Year-round
Other users	Hikers, mountain bikers, equestrians
Map	Anacortes Community Forest Lands Trail Guide

Warm-up

This fun roller-coaster route displays more of the gifts offered by the Anacortes Community Forest Lands (ACFL). Surrounded by dense forest on all sides, Whistle Lake feels like a pond you'd stumble upon somewhere in the Cascade foothills. Some stretches of this route are straight and fast, others are obstacle-course tricky. Be on the watch for mountain bikers; they love ACFL too.

Approach

Take Interstate 5 to exit 230, and head west on Highway 20 for about 11.5 miles to where Highway 20 divides. Take a left, following Highway 20 to Whidbey Island. At **1.8** miles, take a right onto Campbell Lake Road and after 1.6 more miles, a right onto Heart Lake Road. At an unmarked fork 1.3 miles ahead, turn right. Park just ahead at a pullout area/entrance for Mount Erie Road. Elevation: 390 feet.

Go

Find the Sugarloaf Trail sign (Trail 215) and head down the forested single track just to the left of it. (Though a big cedar just to the left sports a Trail 215 sign with a smaller trail next to it, disregard that one. Take the trail that starts immediately to the left of the Sugarloaf sign.) At **0.2** mile, run left and begin a winding, quarter-mile up-and-down jaunt around giant firs and cedars.

Whistle Lake

When the trail merges with Trail 21 (no sign) head to the right and climb an old dirt road. At **0.7** mile, bear left at a clearing and an intersection with an unmarked trail leading to the right. Ignoring trails on either side—some marked, some not—continue straight as the trail widens and becomes flat, then downhill and fast.

At **1.5** miles, run straight onto Trail 22 at the intersection with Trail 21. The wide, easy-to-follow Trail 22 continues descending as it passes through a forested swampy area. At **2.2** miles, check out the abandoned Dodge, right on the trail, sporting tree limbs growing out its windows. Just ahead, take a left at the sign for Whistle Lake. Climbing gently now on Trail 206, make your way up to Toot Swamp and the intersection with Trail 205. Take a right and bear left just ahead at an unmarked fork. Scenic Whistle Lake can be seen through the trees to your left.

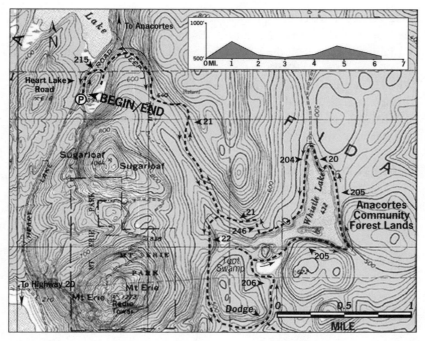

What follows over the next 0.5 mile or so is a roller-coaster/obstacle course with rock, roots, downed and face-level tree trunks providing the impediments. It's fun, but potentially ankle- and noggin-threatening. At **3.2** miles, run left at an intersection and continue on Trail 205. More obstacles follow, along with expansive lake views. About 0.5 mile farther, you'll reach an open area above the lake, perfect for lake-staring and life-contemplating, as well as eating and drinking.

Find Trail 20, a wide route that continues along the lake. Just ahead, bear left onto 204, which continues the lake-hugging behavior. At **4.3** miles, run straight at an intersection, following a sign for Trail 246. Just ahead, you'll reach cool cliff-top views down to the lake. The trail soon merges again with 204. At **4.6** miles, run right at an unmarked T-intersection and after a steep but short climb, take a left onto a wide dirt road that's now a trail. This is Trail 21, which you were on earlier, though not this segment. About 0.25 mile ahead, take a right at the signed intersection with Trail 22 and continue back to your starting point, mostly on Trail 21.

Alternate Routes

See Run #10, Heart Lake–Mount Erie Loop, for the various spots where you can join that route with the Whistle Lake route. For example, run the Heart Lake–Mount Erie Loop to the Sugarloaf Trail (Trail 215) and follow the Whistle Lake route from that point on for a distance of about 9 miles.

You can also follow the Heart Lake–Mount Erie Loop to the intersection of Trails 207 and 21. Take a right on 21 and follow the Whistle Lake route from there for a distance of about 10 miles.

Nearest Support

The Sugarloaf trailhead offers no water or other services. Anacortes Community Forest Lands information, 360/293-1918. Closest food, drink, and places to stay are on Commercial Avenue in Anacortes, about 2 miles north of Heart Lake.

12 Hannegan Peak

PAIN 🏃🏃🏃🏃
GAIN ▲▲▲▲▲

Distance	10.4 miles out and back
Elevation gain	3,050 feet
Time	1.5 to 2.75 hours
The route	Technical and non-technical single track through mountain wilderness. Views. Signs.
Alternate route	20-mile out-and-back route to Copper Mountain lookout.
Runnability	90 percent
Season	July to October
Other users	Hikers
Map	Green Trails Mount Shuksan 14
Permit	Northwest Forest Pass

Warm-up

Eager to sample the many flavors that Cascade Mountain trail running has to offer? Run this route and groove heavily to countless waterfalls tumbling down Nooksack Ridge, thrill as glacier-clad Ruth Mountain seems to expand before your very eyes, get that deep-in-the-heart-of-the-North Cascades

Ruth Mountain and Mount Shuksan from Hannegan Peak

feeling when you reach the top of 6,187-foot Hannegan Peak. This run is a great experience, simple as that.

Approach

From Bellingham head east on Highway 542 (Mount Baker Highway). Continue about 0.5 mile past milepost 46. Turn left on Hannegan Pass Road (Forest Road 32) and continue for about 1.3 miles to a fork. Bear left and reach the road-end parking lot in 4 miles. Elevation: 3,100 feet.

Go

From behind the trailhead map kiosk, head out on a somewhat rocky single track that at first gains almost no elevation. Check out spectacular Nooksack Ridge to the right, Granite Mountain looming overhead, and rushing Ruth Creek creating a commotion in the valley below.

At about **0.6** mile, cross the first of the trail's many creeks. At most of these, expect snow bridges through July, rushing waters through August, and dry creek beds after that. Not far ahead, enter forest for the first time with the trail taking a turn for the rocky and technical. Over the next couple of miles, the views get better with each step as you switch between forest and meadow running. Because you're never deep in the forest, views are never more than a few steps away. Up ahead, Ruth Mountain's single glacier starts to emerge.

At **1.5** miles, hit the trail's first switchback and muscle up a short incline. Soon enough, navigate a gentle ascent while passing through rocky stretches and a number of creeks and creek beds. The trail strikes the phrase "gentle ascent" from its vocabulary list at **3.2** miles, replacing it with the phrase "climb in earnest." You'll gain about 600 feet over the next 0.8 mile. About halfway up this steep section, bear left where the sign for Hannegan Camp urges you right. At **4.0** miles reach Hannegan Pass, a hub for various backpacking and climbing routes in North Cascades National Park. If the mosquitoes and flies allow, take a few moments to eat and drink, or save it for the top of Hannegan Peak—1,100 feet above and 1.2 miles away.

Follow the sign that points north to the peak and start one big lungbuster of a climb. Switchback first through forest, then steep meadow. Mounts Shuksan and Baker present themselves after about 0.5 mile, as do peaks far into British Columbia. After a couple of steep, rocky, and sandy stretches, as well as some likely snow crossings, reach the 6,187-foot summit at **5.2** miles. The 360-degree views of this North Cascades wonderland are truly "the bomb," as

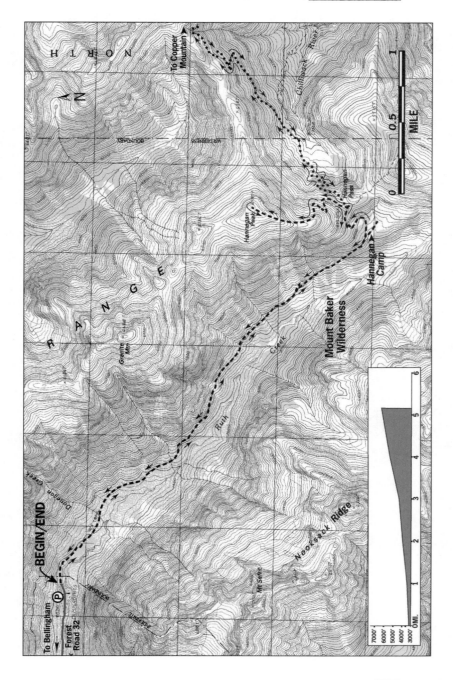

the youth of America likes to say. Low trees on this mini-summit block the wind and make it a great place to replenish.

Return the way you came, taking great care on the steeper sections of the descent.

Alternate Route

For a 20-mile out and back, follow the above description to Hannegan Pass. Once there, follow the sign for Boundary Camp and drop about 700 feet over the next mile until you reach a fork. Run left and continue along Copper Ridge, dropping some, climbing some more, over the next 4 miles. The last mile to the Copper Mountain lookout gains about 1,100 feet. Return the way you came.

Nearest Support

The Hannegan Pass trailhead and Hannegan Pass offer pit toilets but not water. Camping is available at the trailhead and at Silver Fir Campground about 8 miles west of the trailhead on Highway 542. Mount Baker–Snoqualmie National Forest information, 360/856-5700, ext. 515, or www.fs.fed.us/r6/mbs/index.html. Food, drink, and accommodations are available in Glacier, about 20 miles west of the trailhead.

13 Chain Lakes Loop

PAIN 🏃🏃🏃
GAIN ▲▲▲▲▲

Distance	7-mile loop
Elevation gain	1,850 feet
Time	1 to 1.75 hours
The route	Technical and non-technical single track through meadow, forest, and boulder fields. Views. Signs.
Alternate route	14 miles (including 7 miles of out-and-back running along Ptarmigan Ridge).
Runnability	90 percent
Season	August to October
Other users	Hikers
Map	Green Trails Mount Shuksan 14
Permit	Northwest Forest Pass

Warm-up

Today's lesson plan: lakes, blueberries, and boulders, not to mention big-time views of those mega–Mounts—Shuksan and Baker—and one smaller but

Iceberg Lake and Table Mountain

closer massif, Table Mountain. On weekends expect crowds, but with such magic so easily accessible, can you blame them? If the snow level has receded enough, run out Ptarmigan Ridge, where the crowds are smaller but the views will strike your awe.

Approach

Head east on Highway 542 (Mount Baker Highway) almost as far as the road goes (about 55 miles) to the Heather Meadows Visitor Center, about 0.75 mile past the Mount Baker Ski Area's upper lodge. Park in the ample parking lots. Elevation: 4,400 feet.

Go

Begin your run around the base of Table Mountain by finding the Wild Goose Trail and sign at the south end of the upper parking lot. Begin climbing immediately. The trail heads for Artist Point and as such parallels the road part of the way. Check out flat-topped Table Mountain up ahead, broken-topped Mount Shuksan to the left, and Bagley Lakes below and to the right. Herman Saddle, high above the lakes to the west is where you'll emerge once you've made it around Table Mountain.

Following cairns if necessary (depending on the snow level) climb about 600 feet and reach the Artist Point parking lot at about **0.8** mile. Cross the lot, watching out for buses on those late summer/early fall weekends that the lot is free of snow, and follow the sign for Chain Lakes Loop.

Bear to the left—don't head right and up toward the top of Table Mountain—and soon begin a fun, mostly level traverse along the south side of the mountain. Let "Wow!" and "Cool" and even "Gee whiz!" escape your lips, all caused by the super Mount Baker views, which only get better with each step. Some rock slide and creek crossings add variety to this slightly exposed traverse.

At **2.0** miles, run right at the signed intersection with the Ptarmigan Ridge Trail, following the sign for Chain Lakes. Begin dropping quickly and possibly across some lingering snow patches. Pass through a mix of rock gardens, forest, and meadow, losing about 500 feet over the next mile. At **3.0** miles, reach a peaceful spot at the south end of aptly named Iceberg Lake. Eat, drink, and pop some blueberries if they're ripe. Work that upper body, swatting flies and mosquitoes if need be.

Cross a creek or two. After a lazy meander through this mini–lakes district—Hayes and Arbuthnet Lakes also make appearances—start climbing toward Herman Saddle. Follow the sign for Bagley Lakes. At **4.0** miles, after a

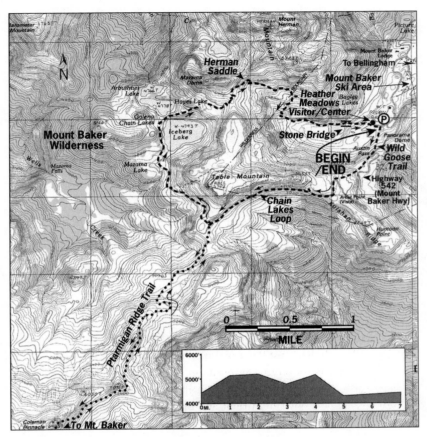

burly climb though forest, rock, and probably a little snow, reach Herman Saddle and its bigger-than-big mountain views. From here, it's almost all downhill, though the sundry rock and boulder fields are likely to prevent you from descending too quickly. Just point your feet toward the lakes down in the basin and have fun.

At **6.5** miles, turn right and cross a stone bridge. Run for the visitor center, about 200 feet above you, and reach your car in about 0.5 mile.

Alternate Route

Follow the above route but at **2.0** miles, run left at the signed intersection with the Ptarmigan Ridge Trail. Continue for 3.5 miles to Coleman Pinnacle—or as far as the snow level allows—for mountain and meadow views among the best anywhere. Return to the Chain Lakes Loop and continue, following the trail description above.

Nearest Support

Heather Meadows Visitor Center offers rest rooms and water but no phones. For the latest conditions, Glacier Public Service Center, 360/599-2714 or www.fs.fed.us/r6/mbs/index.html. The Silver Fir Campground is about 10 miles west of the trailhead on Highway 542 (Mount Baker Highway). More eats and accommodations are available in Glacier, about 20 miles west on Highway 542.

14

MOUNT BAKER HIGHWAY / HIGHWAY 20

Scott Paul Trail

PAIN 🏃🏃🏃

GAIN ▲▲▲▲▲

Distance	8-mile loop
Elevation gain	1,800 feet
Time	1 to 1.75 hours
The route	Soft forest trail to rough moraine. Creek and snow crossings. Signs. Views.
Alternate route	11-mile route that adds side trip to Park Butte and fire lookout.
Runnability	90 percent, depending on snow level
Season	August to October
Other users	Hikers, equestrians
Map	Green Trails Hamilton 45
Permit	Northwest Forest Pass

Warm-up

This fun loop grants you an audience with the glaciers on Mount Baker's south side. Count the crevasses on Baker's icy masses while creek jumping,

Suspension bridge on Scott Paul Trail

gorge crossing, and, more than likely, tiptoeing across mini-snowfields. *Note:* About 3 mostly level miles of the trail are at 5,000 feet, and when I ran this route in early August 2000 I encountered intermittent snow patches beginning at 4,700 feet. Though it required some effort, finding the trail after each snow crossing was fairly easy. Two weeks earlier that wouldn't have been the case. For the latest conditions, call the ranger station or check the Web site.

Approach

Head east on Highway 20 to just past milepost 82, about 15 miles past Sedro Woolley. Turn left on Baker Lake Road. About 12.5 miles farther, turn left on Forest Road 12. In 3 miles, turn right on Forest Road 13 and follow for 6 miles to the road-end parking lot. Elevation: 3,300 feet.

Go

From the trailhead kiosk, run a short way to the Scott Paul Trail sign just before a wood bridge crossing Sulphur Creek. Turn left and cross the bridge though the sign entreats you to run right. (Don't worry, you'll be coming back that way.) After a few hundred yards of boardwalk through peaceful meadow, catch the views to the right of the great white wonder that is Mount Baker. Sherman Peak, the nubbin on the mountain's south side that's a thousand feet lower than the summit, appears Matterhorn-like from this angle.

At **0.8** mile, enter a rocky, creek bed–type area that continues for about 0.5 mile. Cross one of the many creeks you'll encounter on this route via cable suspension bridge at about **1.2** miles. Shortly after, begin climbing steadily and steeply through dense old growth. At **2.0** miles, turn right at a T-intersection following the Scott Paul Trail sign.

The trail soon exits the forest. After traversing wildflower meadows, it veers left and up, entering a glacial moraine environment. What does that mean? Besides spectacular views afforded those who choose—as you do—to lick the toes of Mount Baker's Easton and Squak Glaciers, it means boulders, rocks, snow and creek crossings, and, of course, wet feet. Experience all over the next 3-plus miles.

At **2.7** miles, cross another suspension bridge, this one over the same creek you crossed earlier, albeit here it's in a little more of a rush. Check out Railroad Grade, the massive moraine to your left. Like Mount Baker, it appears to be growing as you run farther north. At **3.5** miles, the trail heads east and promises to soak your feet to the bone over the next 2 miles. Stop from time to time to allow Mount Baker's snowy summit to inspire you.

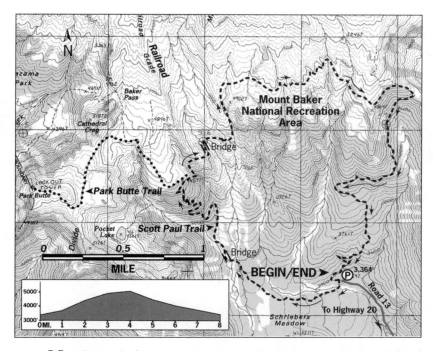

At **5.5** miles, with the mountain views and moraine environment behind you, bear to the right and return to the forest for a rip-roaring 2-plus-mile descent back to the trailhead.

Alternate Route

To add 3 miles and a trip to a fire lookout: At **2.0** miles, run left and follow the sign for the Park Butte Trail. Ignore two trails that lead to the right—one to Railroad Grade (a great side trip in its own right), one to Baker Pass—and reach the lookout after climbing about 700 feet. Return to the Park Butte–Scott Paul Trails intersection and continue on the Scott Paul Trail as described above.

Nearest Support

Pit toilets, but not water, are available at the trailhead. Camping is allowed at the trailhead. Mount Baker–Snoqualmie National Forest information, 360/856-5700, ext. 515, or www.fs.fed.us/r6/mbs/index.html. Nearest food, drink, and accommodations are in Concrete, about 20 miles south of the trailhead off Highway 20.

15 Baker Lake

PAIN 🏃🏃🏃
GAIN ▲▲▲

Distance	14 miles point to point
Elevation gain	400 feet
Time	2 to 3.5 hours
The route	Mostly flat single track and wide trail through lakeside wilderness. Views. Signs.
Runnability	100 percent
Season	Year-round
Other users	Hikers, equestrians
Map	Green Trails Lake Shannon 46
Permit	Northwest Forest Pass

Warm-up

Recent (1999) construction of two bridges has made it possible to run this picturesque trail as a point-to-point journey. On clear days, nearby Mounts Baker and Shuksan poke through the trees at certain points to cheer you on.

Baker River from Baker Lake Trail

Below, Baker Lake beckons for a post-run bellyflop. Take time to admire and be inspired by stretches of old growth timber. Because the trail never goes above 1,000 feet, this is a primo year-round mountain wilderness destination.

Approach

Head east on Highway 20 to just past milepost 82, about 15 miles past Sedro Woolley. Turn left on Baker Lake Road and head north. To park a car where you will finish, drive 26 miles to the road-end parking lot and the Baker River trailhead. To park a car for the start, after about 13 miles on Baker Lake Road, turn right on Forest Road 1106 (Baker Dam Road). Cross Baker Dam in about 1.5 miles and turn left on Forest Road 1107 about 0.3 mile after that. The trailhead is about 0.75 mile ahead on the left. Elevation: 960 feet.

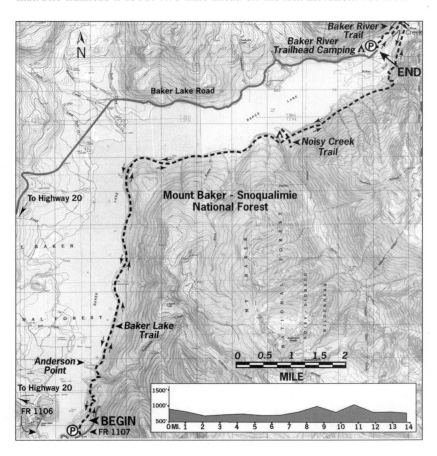

Go

Hop on this deep-forested route and head north for almost 14 miles. A few bumps here and there and streams to cross, but for the most part it's an ever so slightly downhill cruise.

At **1.8** miles, bear right at an intersection with a 0.25-mile trail that heads to the lake at Anderson Point. Continue traversing the lakeside slope for several miles, staying high above the reservoir among some huge trees. Depending on the water level, check out stumps emerging from the bottom of a flooded forest.

Shortly after dropping down close to lakeshore, run straight through a four-way intersection with the Noisy Creek Trail at **8.8** miles. Run the closest thing on this route to a hill over the next 4 miles, perhaps gaining 200 feet before losing it by the time you reach the new wood bridge spanning Blum Creek at about **13.2** miles.

About 200 yards ahead, run left and—speaking of new bridges—cross the spiffy new cable stay bridge spanning the Baker River. Once across, run left at the T-intersection with the Baker River Trail. Reach the Baker River trailhead parking lot in about 0.5 mile at **14.0** miles.

Nearest Support

Pit toilets are available at the Baker River trailhead but not at the Baker Lake trailhead. Several campgrounds are situated along both sides of Baker Lake. Mount Baker–Snoqualmie National Forest information, 360/856-5700, ext. 515, or www.fs.fed.us/r6/mbs/index.html. Nearest food, drink, and accommodations are in Concrete, about 20 miles south of the trailhead off Highway 20.

16 Cascade Pass–Sahale Arm

PAIN 🏃🏃🏃🏃🏃

GAIN ▲ ▲ ▲ ▲ ▲

Distance	12.4 miles out and back
Elevation gain	3,550 feet
Time	1.75 to 3 hours
The route	Technical and non-technical single track and wide trail through mountain wilderness. Views. Signs.
Alternate route	7.4 miles out and back to Cascade Pass.
Runnability	80 percent
Season	July to October
Other users	Hikers
Map	Green Trails Cascade Pass 80
Permit	Northwest Forest Pass

Warm-up

It'd be fun and would nurture the know-it-all inside me to say that popular Cascade Pass is overrated, but you know what? It sure ain't. In fact, the view from the parking lot of massive Johannesburg Mountain is enough to earn it a 5 on the gain scale. Running-wise, it's a nice mix of easy-grade climbing and descending with a couple of stretches that challenge gravity to a tête-a-tête.

Approach

Head east on Highway 20 to Marblemount. Just past milepost 106 turn right onto Cascade River Road and continue for 23 miles, the last 17 on gravel, to the road-end parking lot. Elevation: 3,600 feet.

Go

From the trailhead kiosk, begin by switchbacking through forest on wide, gentle trail that, despite what switchbacks infer—steepness—climbs rather gently. Listen to the myriad waterfalls splashing down Johannesburg as well as the mountain's explosive avalanches. (This is no concern of yours, for Johannesburg Mountain is across the Cascade River Valley.)

Eventually, the switchbacks steepen a little and the trail becomes narrower and adds rocks and roots by the barrelful. Basically, the route to Cascade Pass is

Climbing toward Cascade Pass-Sahale

2.5 miles of forest switchbacks, followed by 1.2-mile traverse across meadow and scree slopes to the Pass. It's accompanied, of course, by those mountain views—Johannesburg has the lead, but the stellar supporting cast includes Cascade Peak, the Triplets, and behind you, Eldorado Peak.

At **3.7** miles reach Cascade Pass and run left at a T-intersection, following the sign for Stehekin. Just ahead turn right. About 20 yards after that, run left at the sign for Sahale Arm. Begin an extremely steep, rocky, slippery climb that gets you some sky in a hurry—about 700 feet in 0.75 mile. At **4.4** miles, crest a ridge and gaze in wonder at Sahale Mountain straight ahead—lotsa rock, lotsa glaciers. Here is a great place to eat and drink before heading up some more. Better yet, save it for the way down.

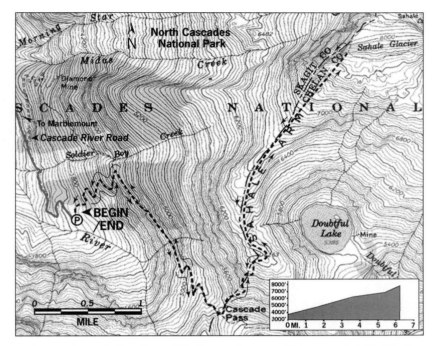

Ignore the trail that drops 800 feet to the emerald waters of chilly Doubt-ful Lake and instead run left and up the meadows of Sahale Arm as far as the snow level allows. Views approach mega-view status as Glacier and Forbidden Peaks swing into view. If you can make it that far, turn around at the edge of Sahale Glacier, at **6.2** miles, and return the way you came.

Alternate Route
For about 1,500 fewer feet of climbing and perhaps 80 percent of the views, turn around at Cascade Pass.

Nearest Support
Pit toilets are available at the Cascade Pass trailhead and at Cascade Pass, though water is not. Camping is available at the trailhead and at various camp-grounds on Cascade River Road. North Cascades National Park information, 360/873-4590 or www.nps.gov/noca. For food, drink, and places to stay, Marblemount is 23 miles west of the trailhead.

17

Mountain Lake to Mount Constitution

PAIN 🏃🏃🏃

GAIN ▲▲▲▲▲

Distance	8.4-mile lollipop loop
Elevation gain	1,850 feet
Time	1.25 to 2.25 hours
The route	Wide, level forested trail and long steep climb. One of the Northwest's best vistas. Signs.
Alternate route	3.9-mile loop with almost no elevation gain.
Runnability	80 percent
Season	Year-round
Other users	Hikers, mountain bikers, except in summer
Maps	Moran State Park Map and Trail Guide; USGS Mount Constitution (7.5' series)

Warm-up

From the top of Mount Constitution, it seems possible to leap out and land on the snowy summit of Mount Baker, on a street in downtown Vancouver, B.C., or on any of the surrounding islands. Views from Constitution's summit are among the Northwest's best—and this route makes you earn them.

Approach

From Anacortes, take the Washington State Ferry to Orcas Island. Once there, drive 9 miles on Orcas Road (Horseshoe Highway) to Eastsound. Continue through town and about 1 mile farther, turn right on Olga Road. Follow this road for 3.2 miles to the Moran State Park entrance archway. In 1.3 miles, turn left at the fork and follow signs for the Mount Constitution summit. A little more than a mile farther, take a right at the sign for Mountain Lake. The parking lot is about 0.25 mile ahead. Elevation: 920 feet.

Go

On the lake side of the parking lot, find the well-marked Mountain Lake Loop Trail and follow to the right. The route follows the lake's perimeter for almost 3 miles. For the first stretch, keep the lake to your left and ignore any

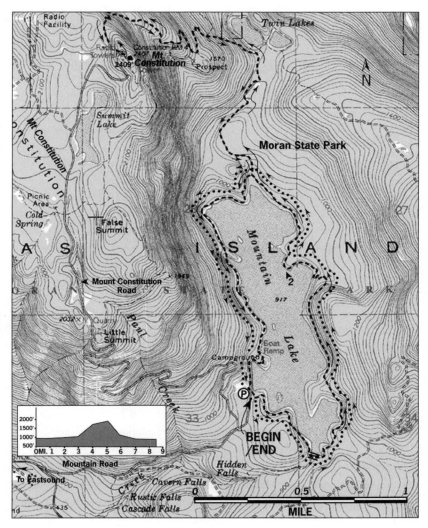

trails leading to the right.

At about **0.5** mile, near the southern tip of the lake, cross a bridge by a dam and pick up the trail on the other side. Bear left at an intersection just ahead. Follow the lake shoreline while luxuriating in the wide, wide trail, admiring the big ol' cedars and firs, and scanning the sky for the occasional osprey circling the lake. No single track on this route, thank you.

At about **2.8** miles, take your first right, following the sign for Twin Lakes and bidding Mountain Lake adieu for now. Make note of this intersection: You'll be back. Climb a little over the next 0.7 of a mile, just enough to let you know that you've left the flat stuff behind you. At **3.5** miles, with Twin Lakes directly ahead of you, run left at the sign for Mount Constitution and start fighting gravity. Ignore two trails to the right over the next 0.3 mile. As the sign at the second intersection tells you, it's 1.2 miles to the summit. What it doesn't tell you is that it's almost 1,200 more feet to the top.

The trail meanders, switchbacks, heads straight up in sections—pretty much tries it all, but it's still what those in the industry call a grind. Just think though, especially on those long, straight, steep stretches, what the downhill is going to be like: your fastest mile ever. At about **4.9** miles, the grade lessens and with more sky poking through the trees, you can be sure that the top is near. You're right. Less than 0.25 mile ahead, pop out onto a paved loop parking lot—pity those folk who drove cars to get here—and head for the stone tower and vista just ahead.

The view's quality has been calculated as follows: Wow!-squared. Double that quantity. Multiply that by pi. Square that quantity. Now quadruple-square it. And that's on cloudy days. 'Nuff sed. Sprint like a schoolgirl or boy to the top of the stone tower. You'll be so distracted by the views you won't even notice the protestations of your quads and hammies. As if all this wasn't enough, water and rest rooms are available up top too.

When you've had your fill, return the way you came for about 2.3 miles to the northern tip of Mountain Lake. This time, continue straight through, bearing to the right and following the sign for the Mountain Lake Campground. From here, it's a mostly level cruise back to the parking lot. At **8.3** miles, turn right on a dirt road when you reach the campground. The parking lot is just ahead.

Alternate Route

The scenic 3.9-mile loop around Mountain Lake has almost no elevation gain. Follow the trail description above, but at **2.8** miles, instead of taking a right for Twin Lakes, run straight., finishing where you started.

Nearest Support

The trailhead parking lot offers water and rest rooms. Moran State Park boasts several campgrounds. Park information, 360/376-2326 or www.parks.wa.gov/moran.htm. The town of Eastsound, about 5 miles away, offers much in the way of food, drink, and accommodations. Washington State Ferry schedule and rates, 888/808-7977 or www.wsdot.wa.gov/ferries.

18

SAN JUAN ISLANDS

Mount Constitution/ Pickett Loop

PAIN 🏃🏃🏃🏃

GAIN ▲ ▲ ▲ ▲

Distance	13-mile loop
Elevation gain	3,200 feet
Time	1.75 to 3 hours
The route	Wide trails to tricky technical single track. Steep climbs, fast descents. Views. Well-signed.
Runnability	80 percent
Season	Year-round
Other users	Hikers, mountain bikers, except in summer
Maps	Moran State Park Map and Trail Guide; USGS Mount Constitution (7.5' series)

Warm-up

Run this route and you'll be whooped, but you'll also have experienced a little of everything that wonderful Moran State Park has to offer: the spectacular view from atop Mount Constitution, deep forests, mountain lakes, sparkling waterfalls, and more. Running-wise, you've got long, steep climbs and super-fast descents, as well as a great ridge run.

Approach

From Anacortes, take the Washington State Ferry to Orcas Island. Once there, drive 9 miles on Orcas Road to Eastsound. Continue through town. About 1 mile farther, take a right on Olga Road. Take this road for 3.2 miles to the Moran State Park entrance archway. The Cold Springs trailhead is about 0.4 mile ahead on the left. Elevation: 370 feet.

Go

Head up the well-marked Cold Springs Trail and begin climbing through forest immediately. Though the trail climbs more than 1,600 feet in little more than 2 miles, its multiple switchbacks take some of the steep out of what is a fairly relentless ascent. Expect wet feet as the trail crisscrosses creeks in several spots.

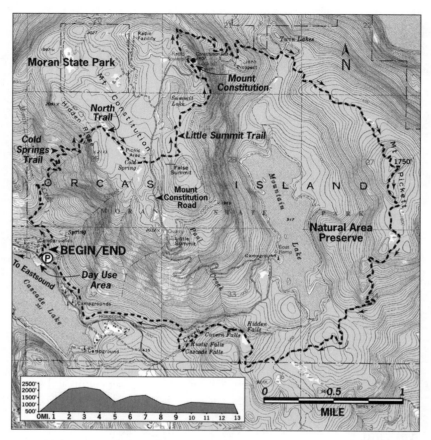

At 1.7 miles, reach a minor meadow area where the first views open up to the south. Check out some of the other San Juans and the mainland before passing back into the woods. Continue climbing until a signed intersection with the North Trail at 2.3 miles. With the worst of the climbing behind you, run straight over a flat, wide trail and follow the sign for Tower. About 0.5 mile farther, after passing a couple of shelters, come to paved Mount Constitution Road. Cross over and pick up the trail on the other side, following the sign for Mount Constitution.

Pass through a forested swamp area and at 3.3 miles take a left at a T-intersection. Follow the sign for the lookout tower and pass through a stretch of skinny lodgepole pine. Soon, stunning ridge-top views open up to the right— mountains, islands, all of northern Puget Sound. The view from the top of

Mount Constitution is one of the best anywhere, and these are just about as good and accompany you for about 0.5 mile. Check out Mount Pickett in the foreground to the east. You'll be there in a half hour or so.

At **4.3** miles, reach the top of Mount Constitution. Eat, drink, gawk, refill your water bottles, use the rest room if you have to, then find the trailhead to Twin Lakes on the far side of the Mount Constitution parking lot and head down.

It's a shame you quickly lose much of the elevation you worked so hard to gain, but such is life as a trail runner. At **5.5** miles, having dropped more than 1,100 feet in little more than a mile, continue straight at an intersection, following the sign for Mountain Lake. About 0.3 mile ahead, and 300 feet lower, run left at a four-way intersection. Follow the sign for Mount Pickett.

After crossing a wood bridge, run along one of the Twin Lakes for about 100 yards. Just before crossing a creek that connects the two lakes, take a hard right. Hug the stately fir that's right there on your right if you have to. Start the gradual forested climb up Mount Pickett, first on single track, eventually on an abandoned dirt road given to mud during the rainy season. After the major climb and descent your quads and hammies went through earlier, this climb is likely to seem steeper than it really is. (Some comfort, huh?)

At **7.5** miles, reach the summit of Mount Pickett. No views, just a sign, but hey, Mount Constitution has enough views for ten summits. (Some comfort, huh?) Good place to eat and drink before a long descent. Once back on the run, begin dropping elevation almost immediately. In about 0.75 mile, reach a wetlands area and run along the park's Natural Area Preserve, the largest unlogged forest tract in the Puget Sound trough.

Run straight at an intersection at **9.5** miles following the sign for Cascade Falls. (Cascade Falls is your immediate destination, so if in doubt over the next 2 miles or so, follow signs for Cascades Falls.) Ascend for a short stretch before resuming what has been a fairly long descent. At **10.5** miles, continue straight at an intersection and reach an open area that appears to serve as a park refuse area—with lots of used picnic tables, sign posts, and the like.

About 0.25 mile ahead, turn left at the Cascade Falls sign and drop quickly down to a creek on a winding single track. At **11.3** miles, run straight at a signed intersection but remember this spot for you'll be back in two shakes.

Check out Cascade Falls a few hundred yards ahead on your left. Take a gander, take a drink, then return to the signed intersection you just passed. This time run left and up, reaching a parking area in about 100 yards. Cross Mount

Constitution Road and pick up the signed single track on the other side. From here it's a 1.7-mile winding roller-coaster jog back to where you started.

Nearest Support

Cold Springs trailhead offers water, phones, and rest rooms. Moran State Park boasts several campgrounds. Park information, 360/376-2326 or www.parks. wa.gov/moran.htm. The town of Eastsound, about 3 miles away, offers much in the way of food, drink, and accommodations. For Washington State Ferry schedule and rates, 888/808-7977 or out www.wsdot.wa.gov/ferries.

19

SAN JUAN ISLANDS

Cascade Lake Loop

PAIN 🏃

GAIN ▲ ▲

Distance	2.7-mile loop
Elevation gain	350 feet
Time	20 to 40 minutes
The route	Wide dirt trail and single track around lake. Minor rolling hills through forest. Some signs.
Runnability	100 percent
Season	Year-round
Other users	Hikers
Maps	Moran State Park Map and Trail Guide; USGS Mount Constitution (7.5' series)

Warm-up

Not every trail run in Moran State Park is a gravity fighter. This one is a mostly gentle loop around Cascade Lake that explores the park's lower region. It's a nice alternative to the other Orcas Island routes in this guide.

Gnarled fir over Cascade Lake

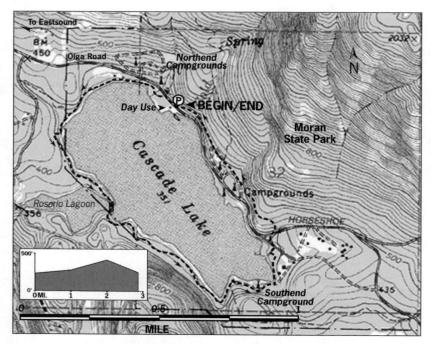

Approach

From Anacortes, take the Washington State Ferry to Orcas Island. Once there, drive 9 miles on Orcas Road (Horseshoe Highway) to Eastsound. Continue through town. About 1 mile farther, turn right on Olga Road. Take this road for 3.2 miles to the Moran State Park entrance archway. The Cascade Lake Day Use Area is about 0.4 mile ahead on the right. Elevation: 350 feet.

Go

From the day use area, follow the sign for Cascade Lake Loop and run down the wide, easy-to-follow trail. At **0.4** mile, take note of a weird, twisted Douglas fir growing out over the lake and doing its best madrone impression. Just ahead, veer left at a four-way intersection and follow the sign for the campground.

At **1.0** mile, cross a wood bridge while passing Rosario Lagoon on your right. The trail now narrows at times and becomes somewhat rocky, but nothing too technical. At **1.6** miles, just after a bike barricade, continue straight into South End Campground. Just ahead, hop on a paved campground road for about 150 yards before taking a left on the first trail you come to.

Resume following the lakeshore for about 200 yards. Just after the trail leaves the shoreline, run left at an unmarked intersection, and 50 yards later run right onto a paved road. In another 50 yards, run left at the intersection with the paved park office road. In less than half a shake, follow the sign to the right for the trail. After crossing Olga Road, follow the Cascade Lake Loop sign.

Begin a short climb and at **1.9** miles run left at a T-intersection, following the sign for a picnic area. From here it's a gentle winding and roller-coaster 0.8-mile jog back to the day use area.

Nearest Support

Cascade Lake Day Use Area offers water, phones, and rest rooms. Moran State Park boasts several campgrounds. Park information, 360/376-2326 or www.parks.wa.gov/moran.htm. The town of Eastsound, about 3 miles away offers much in the way of food, drink, and accommodations. Washington State Ferry schedule and rates, 888/808-7977 or www.wsdot.wa.gov/ferries.

20

EVERETT

Spencer Island

PAIN 🏃
GAIN 🔺🔺

Distance	3.6-mile lollipop loop
Elevation gain	30 feet
Time	30 to 50 minutes
The route	Flat, gentle run on wide dirt path. Well-signed.
Runnability	100 percent
Season	Year-round
Other users	Hikers
Maps	USGS Everett, USGS Marysville (both 7.5' series)

Warm-up

This easy marsh run doubles as a bird-watching outing. Herons, hawks, and waterfowl galore populate this scenic wetlands area. The wide dirt and wood chip trail is as easy on the joints as the wildlife is on the eyes. Beware during winter months, however. Hunters do the pow! pow! thing on the northern half of the island.

Approach

From Interstate 5, take exit 195 in Everett. Head north on East Marine View Drive for 1.5 miles to Highway 529. Bear right. After crossing a bridge spanning the Snohomish River, take the first right, following signs for Langus Riverfront Park. After 0.3 mile, take a left onto Ross Avenue, and 0.8 mile after that bear right at a fork onto Smith Island Road. (Left crosses over the freeway.) Continue for more than a mile to the road's end, passing under the freeway and ignoring the various waste treatment-plant turnoffs on either side of the road. Park at the small gravel parking lot. Elevation: 10 feet.

Go

From the parking lot, head east on the gravel road. After about 0.3 mile, cross a bridge onto Spencer Island. After taking a moment at the interpretive board and map to familiarize yourself with the route and determine whether or not it's hunting season, take a right and head south on the wide, gravel road. You'll be running a 3-mile loop tracing the perimeter of the island, so feel free to let

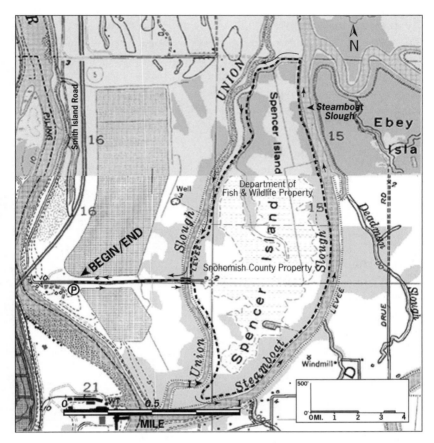

your trail-running mind wander. Soon the gravel road gives way to a super-wide, super-soft dirt and wood chip trail.

At **1.2** miles, continue straight at an intersection where the main trail appears to head left. A sign at **1.6** miles states, "License Required"—hunting license, that is. You've now crossed into the Department of Fish and Wildlife section of Spencer Island. Keep running the obvious trail, perhaps a little less obvious (but no less soft) in a couple of overgrown spots.

Leave the Fish and Wildlife section at about **3.0** miles and about 0.3 mile ahead, complete the loop by returning to the bridge and interpretive board. Run back to the parking lot the way you came or add another lap or two if you're in the mood for more mileage.

Nearest Support

The Spencer Island trailhead offers no services, though there is a portable toilet 0.3 mile into the route at the map and interpretive board. Snohomish County Parks and Recreation Department, 425/388-6600 or www.co.snohomish.wa.us/parks/spencer.htm. Everett, fewer than 3 miles away, offers much in food, drink, and accommodations.

21 | EVERETT
Mount Pilchuck

PAIN 🏃🏃🏃
GAIN 🔺🔺🔺🔺

Distance	6 miles out and back
Elevation gain	2,100 feet
Time	50 minutes to 1.5 hours
The route	Technical single track through forest and boulder fields. Views. No signs.
Runnability	80 percent
Season	July to October
Other users	Hikers
Map	Green Trails Granite Falls 109
Permit	Northwest Forest Pass

Warm-up

Short, but steep, Mount Pilchuck packs a ton of running challenges in these 6 miles out and back. The trail throws in the requisite rocks and roots as well as a couple of miles of granite boulders and rocky gardens. Because it's easy to

Mountain views from Mount Pilchuck

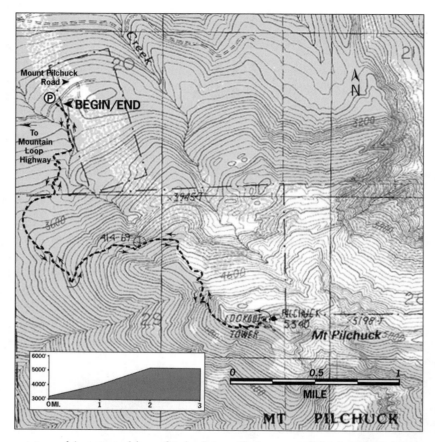

get to and is crowned by a fire lookout offering one of the best 360-degree vistas anywhere, Mount Pilchuck is not a place where you'll be overcome by loneliness, but the views might get you.

Approach

From the Mountain Loop Highway in Granite Falls, drive east about 12 miles to Mount Pilchuck Road. Turn right and continue for 7 miles to the trailhead parking lot. Elevation: 3,100 feet.

Go

Begin this somewhat relentless climb by running up the rock- and root-studded trail that heads up into stately old growth. After crossing a definite "wet foot" creek, begin a series of switchbacks. At **0.6** mile, cross through a clearcut area that offers a hint of the views that are to be had in great abundance. Soon the trail returns to dense forest before opening up and offering hints of something else that's to come: boulder fields that dominate much of the route.

Views improve the higher you run and so does the rock and potential injury quotient. Concentration is key to keeping a twisted ankle from being your only memory of this route—especially on the return when you'll be maneuvering downhill through these rocks.

At **1.6** miles, reach a flat area that offers a chance to catch your breath and some impressive views of the North Cascades. About 0.25 mile ahead, enter an open area with huge, exposed rock slabs. Pilchuck's rocky upper reaches loom high above, seemingly directly overhead. Give a good squint and you'll spot the fire lookout—at the end of the mission you've chosen to accept. At **2.2** miles, the trail climbs along the west and south sides of the mountain, opening up cans of Rainier and Olympic Mountain views.

Continue climbing through a mix of boulder field and forest until you reach the top (5,340 feet) at **3.0** miles. The final 25 feet to the lookout require a scramble up giant boulders and a short climb up a ladder. Views are all-encompassing—the volcanoes, Olympics, Puget Sound, plus the plethora of lowland towns, burgs, villages, and hamlets.

Return the way you came, reminding yourself that you only have one pair of ankles and knees. If you're in a burly mood, do another up and down.

Nearest Support

Pit toilets are the only trailhead support. Mount Baker–Snoqualmie National Forest information, 360/436-1155 or www.fs.fed.us/r6/mbs/index.html. Food, drink, and accommodations are available in Granite Falls, about 20 miles west of the trailhead.

22

EVERETT
Wallace Falls State Park

PAIN 🏃🏃🏃

GAIN ▲▲▲▲

Distance	7.6 miles out and back
Elevation gain	1,300 feet
Time	1 to 1.75 hours
The route	Technical single track and old railroad grade along the tumbling Wallace River. Views. Well-signed.
Alternate route	12.8-mile route that adds 5.2 miles out and back to Wallace Lake.
Runnability	90 percent
Season	Year-round
Other users	Hikers
Map	Green Trails Index 142

Warm-up

This route's draw are the waterfalls, and if you run here on weekends you'll realize that lots of people feel that way. Though the trail saves the steepest, most technical running for near the top, the best views of the falls are fairly low. The route offers many places to stare at the plunging water while you water and feed yourself.

Approach

From Everett, take Highway 2 east for about 30 miles to Gold Bar. Turn left on First Street and follow signs for about 2 miles to Wallace Falls State Park. Elevation: 350 feet.

Go

Find the trailhead kiosk, look the map over once or twice, sign the register if you like, and head up the obvious trail. After passing below some daunting power lines, enter the forest. At **0.5** mile, take a right on the Woody Trail, passing through a bike barricade as you do. (You'll be returning via the railroad-grade trail on the left, so remember this spot.)

Dip down momentarily, cross a bridge, and after a short climb begin running along the Wallace River. Rocks and roots along the trail will keep you on your toes—literally, at times. At **1.5** miles, take note of—but don't take—

the railroad-grade trail which intersects to the left. On the way back, you'll turn right here.

About 0.3 mile farther, near a pleasant picnic shelter, catch the first really good glimpse of the falls. Switchback up an increasingly technical stretch of trail—rocks and roots are strewn about like a child's toys across a rec-room floor—and at **2.3** miles, stop to gape and gawk at the tumbling rumble of water.

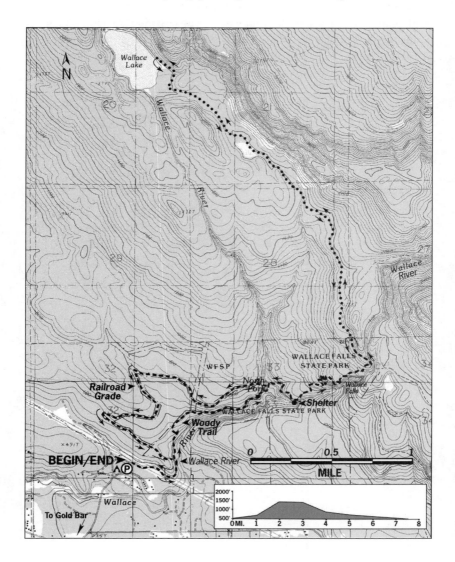

At 265 feet, this horsetail of whitewater falls is only 5 feet less than Snoqualmie Falls.

Continue a steep rockin' and rootin' 0.5 mile to another viewpoint, this one boasting views to the Skykomish Valley and Olympic Mountains. At **3.3** miles, reach the last of the four viewpoints, this one offering two impressive plunges, though they are much smaller than the main falls.

Return the way you came until you get to the railroad-grade trail. Take a right, adding about a mile to your return but lessening the descent's steep quotient and your chances of a twisted or broken ankle from those pesky rock 'n' roots. Connect back with the trail about 0.5 mile from the parking lot and return to your starting point the way you came.

Alternate Route

From the final viewpoint, continue on the sometimes hard-to-follow trail for about 2.6 miles to Wallace Lake. Return the way you came. This adds 5.2 miles to your run.

Nearest Support

Wallace State Park offers water, rest rooms, and phones. Park information, 360/793-0420 or www.parks.wa.gov/wallacef.htm. The park also offers camping. Gold Bar is 2 miles away and offers more in the way of food, drinks, and accommodations.

23 Iron Goat Trail

PAIN 🏃🏃

GAIN ▲ ▲ ▲

Distance	11.4 miles out and back
Elevation gain	720 feet
Time	1.5 to 2.75 hours
The route	Forested single track and wide trail on old railroad grade. 1.2 miles of tunnel. Views.
Alternate route	5.7 miles point to point
Runnability	100 percent
Season	April to November
Other users	Hikers
Map	Green Trails Stevens Pass 176
Permit	Northwest Forest Pass

Warm-up

This trail offers a lesson on the Northwest's railroad history. Passing several abandoned tunnels and snowsheds, the route follows the old Great Northern Railway tracks that crossed Stevens Pass more than a hundred years ago. The

Remains of a snowshed on Iron Goat Trail

Iron Goat gains roughly 125 feet in elevation per mile, which is hardly notice-able on the out part of this out and back. On the back part, however, you'll feel like someone's giving you a gentle push all the way.

Approach

Head east on Highway 2 to just past milepost 55. Turn left onto the Old Cas-cade Highway and follow the sign for the Iron Goat Trail. In 2.3 miles, turn left on Forest Road 6710, a dirt road, and continue for 1.4 miles to the Mar-tin Creek trailhead. Elevation: 2,500 feet.

Go

From the trailhead kiosk, run south on the wood plank trail that soon becomes a wide gravel path. In about 200 yards run left and up, following the sign for Martin Creek Crossover. This narrow, rocky stretch climbs for a few hundred yards but is the steepest ascent of the trail. Just after the trail levels out, take note of the jumble of logs, all that remains of snowsheds built to hold back avalanches when the railroad was being built. They look like lava flows made out of wood.

At **0.5** mile, pass the first of several abandoned tunnels. Feel free to look, but as the interpretive signs tell you, don't enter. About 0.25 mile ahead, run left at a fork in the trail. At **1.4** miles, cross one of the many creeks that inter-sect the trail and have the potential to be real gushers in spring and early sum-mer. Just ahead, ignore a trail leading to the right.

At **1.6** miles, run along a number of concrete walls, the remains of a reser-voir and spillway from the railroad's past. Lots of water still spills its way over the top these days, so expect wet feet. Central Cascade views open up to the right at **2.0** miles and continue on and off for the rest of the trail. Look down at what appear to be toy cars and eighteen-wheelers on Highway 2. Just ahead, pass another tunnel, taking care as you maneuver along a rocky stretch that follows.

In about 0.5 mile, the narrow top of a spillway wall is followed by a jumble of boulders. At **3.0** miles, the Windy Point Tunnel offers a nice place to stop to sip something cool. Just ahead, for those in need, an open-air privy overlook-ing Highway 2 offers a true loo with a view. (Ouch.) About 0.75 mile ahead, pass the twisted molten-looking remains of another shed. Bizarre.

At **5.1** miles, enter a 0.6-mile snowshed/tunnel that's open to the right. The wide dirt path is great fun to run on, and the tunnel roof protects from the elements. Make chugga-chugga-wooo-wooo! sounds and pretend you're a

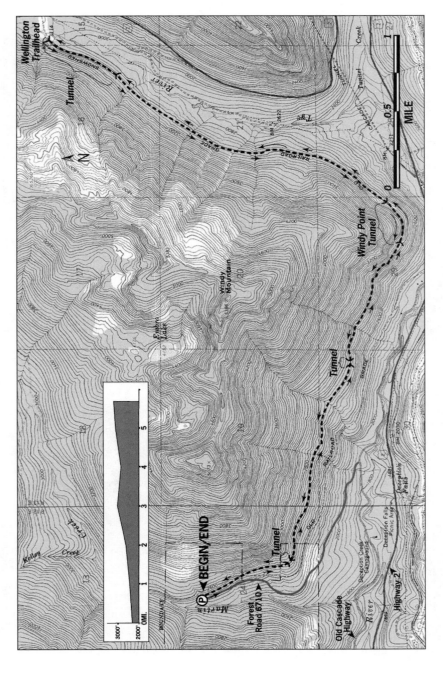

train. It seems fitting. At **5.7** miles, leave the tunnel and come to the Wellington trailhead. After hydrating, which is fancy pants-ese for drinking, reenter the tunnel and return the way you came.

Alternate Route

To run this trail as a 5.7-mile, point-to-point route, park one car at the Wellington trailhead and the other at the Martin Creek trailhead. For a downhill take on the trail, start at the Wellington trailhead.

Nearest Support

Portable toilets are available at both ends of the Iron Goat Trail and at about the midway point. No other support is offered. Iron Goat Trail information, 206/283-1440 or www.bcc.ctc.edu/cpsha/irongoat/default.htm. Skykomish, which offers food, drink, and lodging, is about 10 miles west on Highway 2.

24

SEATTLE / BELLEVUE

St. Edward State Park

PAIN 🏃🏃

GAIN ▲▲

Distance	3.5-mile loop
Elevation gain	780 feet
Time	25 to 45 minutes
The route	Well-maintained trails offering soft landings through magical urban wilderness. Lakeshore views. Well-signed.
Runnability	100 percent
Season	Year-round
Other users	Hikers
Map	St. Edward State Park (available in park office near north parking lot)

Warm-up

Don't let the no-nonsense, Romanesque brick buildings of St. Edward State Park mislead you. Surrounding this one-time seminary are 316 acres of forest wilderness, as well as 3,000 feet of Lake Washington shoreline. About 6 miles of trails crisscross the park, including some impressive steeps that make for challenging climbs and let-the-good-times-roll descents.

Approach

From Interstate 405, take exit 23 and head west on Highway 522 for about 4 miles. Turn left onto 68th Avenue NE, which eventually becomes Juanita Drive NE. Head south about 1.5 miles. The park entrance is on the right. Follow signs to the right for the north parking lot. Elevation: 330 feet.

Go

From the parking lot, follow the sign for the wide, spacious North Trail. The trail drops quickly into a deep fir forest, then runs high above a creek. Continue dropping steadily, about 330 feet by the time you reach the lakeshore at **0.7** mile.

Bear to the left and run along the lake for about 0.5 mile. At **1.2** miles, arrive at an open area with the Grotto Trail leading to your left. Don't follow, but make note for you'll be returning here. Continue along the lake for a few

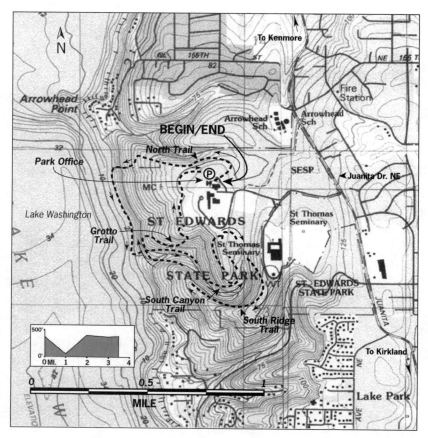

yards and arrive at the South Canyon Trail. Run left on South Canyon, which, despite its moderate rating, climbs fairly steadily—though not as steeply as the Grotto Trail, which you can see climbing above you to the left.

At **1.8** miles, the trail merges with the Orchard Loop. Bear right and exit the forest in about 0.25 mile just beyond a mountain-bike–unfriendly wood barricade. Run to the right at this somewhat vague lawn area and spot a trail sign and dirt road entrance (Water Tower Road) a few hundred yards farther on. Head down Water Tower, ignoring trail spurs on either side. After narrowing and climbing a small hill, what is now the trail comes to a signed T at **2.2** miles. Take a right following the arrow for the South Ridge Trail.

Put 'er in cruise control and over the next 0.6 mile, let gravity be your engine as you drop 400 feet back to the lake. Except for one narrow, tiptoe-worthy stretch just before the intersection with the South Canyon Trail, the route is a wide, dirt path offering a soft landing.

Run past the South Canyon entrance, returning instead to the open area at the foot of the Grotto Trail at **2.9** miles. Turn right. A few yards ahead, past privies on either side of the trail, take a right on the Grotto Trail. Work up a sweat on this last ascent, which climbs about 300 feet over the next 0.5 mile. At **3.4** miles, just beyond a no-bikes barricade, emerge from the forest behind the former seminary building. Stay to the left and run the perimeter of the park's lawn, ducking back into the forest for one stretch, back to the north parking lot.

Nearest Support

St. Edward Park offers rest rooms, water, and phones. Park information, 425/823-2992 or www.parks.wa.gov/sainted.htm. Kenmore's Highway 522 is about 1.5 miles north and is the site of numerous restaurant and motel choices.

25 Discovery Park Loop

PAIN 🏃

GAIN ▲ ▲ ▲

Distance	3.3-mile loop
Elevation gain	520 feet
Time	30 to 50 minutes
The route	Wide gravel and dirt trails through forest and meadow. Sandy beach. Views. Signs.
Runnability	100 percent
Season	Year-round
Other users	Hikers
Map	Discovery Park map (available at visitor center)

Warm-up

Seattle's largest park offers so many distractions you'll find yourself repeatedly hitting the stop button on your watch. Soak in the awesome bluff-top views of Puget Sound and the Olympic Mountains. Run along the sandy beach and check out West Point Lighthouse, built in 1881. This route mainly follows the park's Loop Trail, with a beach detour thrown in.

Approach

From Interstate 5, take exit 169. Head west on 45th Street, bearing right as it becomes NW Market Street, to 15th Avenue NW. Turn left. After crossing the Ballard Bridge, take the West Dravus exit. Turn right onto 20th Avenue W and follow this road as it curves to the left, becoming Gilman Avenue W, then West Government Way, and eventually entering the park. (Follow signs for Discovery Park.) Park at the visitor center, your first left upon entering the park. Elevation: 210 feet.

Go

From the visitor center, run across the parking lot and find the brown trail marker that points the way to the Discovery Park Loop Trail 300 feet ahead. After a short climb up a wide gravel path, run left into the forest, following the Loop Trail marker. Follow these signed trail markers throughout as the trail crosses a number of roads, paths, parking lots, and more.

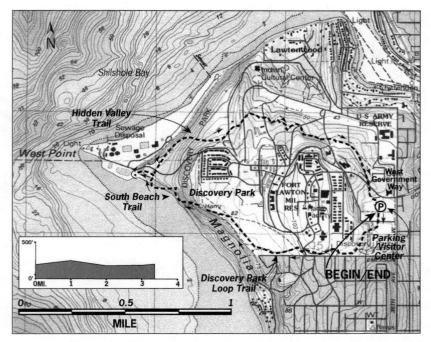

After about a 0.5-mile warm-up through forest, the trail wends its way through an open meadow area. Listen as the phrase "windswept" pops into your head. At **0.9** mile, after passing one of the loop's many rest rooms, the trail veers right and runs along the top of a 200-foot cliff. Take a moment to gawk at the regal Olympic Mountains staring back at you from across Puget Sound. Follow the now-sandy trail as it follows a cliff-side barricade. At **1.2** miles, leave the Loop Trail and run left, following the sign for South Beach Trail. Descend quickly down a dirt path and wood steps through forest for a few hundred yards and take another left, again following the South Beach Trail sign.

Continue descending and just ahead, at **1.5** miles, take a right and run 100 yards to a road. Run left and head down to the beach, about 200 yards away. If so inclined, turn the stopwatch off and run up or down the beach, with the wind in your hair and all that. West Point Lighthouse is about 0.25 mile up the beach to the right. A sewage disposal plant sits just beyond that. Neat.

Resume your running loop by heading back up the paved trail and taking a left at the first crosswalk. (You came from the right just moments before.) Follow the sign for North Bluff (the map calls this the Hidden Valley Trail). After a gently climbing jaunt through some woods, at **2.2** miles run straight through an intersection, following the sign for the Loop Trail and North Parking Lot. Just ahead, rejoin the Loop Trail. Cross several paved service and park roads, following signs for the Loop Trail and/or the visitor center each time.

At **3.3** miles, just after running under a bridge for the main park road, complete the loop. The visitor center parking lot is 100 yards to your left.

Nearest Support

The Discovery Park visitor center offers rest rooms, water, and telephones. Park information, 206/386-4236 or www.ci.seattle.wa.us/parks/Environment/discovparkindex.htm. The park is located in Seattle's Magnolia neighborhood, which offers plenty in the food, drink, and accommodations department.

SEATTLE / BELLEVUE

26 Washington Park Arboretum

PAIN 🏃

GAIN ▲ ▲

Distance	2.8-mile out and back
Elevation gain	120 feet
Time	20 to 40 minutes.
The route	Wide gravel paths, floating cement bridges, and soft trail through urban park and marshlands. Signs.
Runnability	100 percent
Season	Year-round
Other users	Hikers
Map	Arboretum Trail (available in the visitor center)

Warm-up

The University of Washington's 230-acre arboretum offers a maze of trails on which you not only can get a workout, but also can brush up on your plants. Many trees, shrubs, and other green and growing things wear small tags telling their phylum and genus. The following route leads to the Montlake Cut and offers a glimpse into Seattle's boating life.

Husky Stadium from a floating bridge on the Arboretum trail

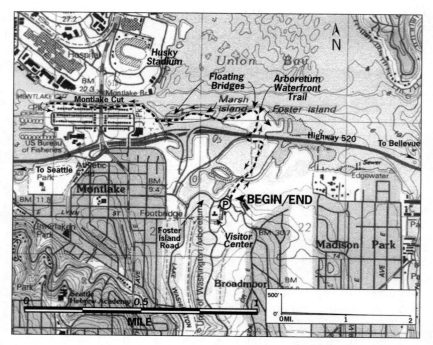

Approach

From Highway 520 east, take the Lake Washington Boulevard exit; from Highway 520 west, take the Montlake exit. Once off the exits, turn left and then left again onto Foster Island Road, following the sign for the visitor center. Turn right onto Arboretum Drive in about 0.25 mile. The visitor center parking lot is just ahead on the left. Elevation: 50 feet.

Go

From the visitor center parking lot, run right onto Arboretum Drive, then right again onto Foster Island Road. Continue for a few hundred yards until the pavement ends and pick up the wide gravel path. At **0.4** mile, pass under the freeway. Just ahead, run left at a fork following the sign for the Arboretum Waterfront Trail.

Pass through a waterfront marshy area on a bouncy dirt and wood chip path. Soon, cross a metal grating and concrete floating bridge that puts you level with thousands of ducks and lily pads, as well as kayakers and canoeists. Look across Union Bay to Husky Stadium—and if it's a Saturday afternoon in the fall, give a cheer for the old Purple and Gold.

At **0.7** mile, land on aptly named Marsh Island. About 0.25 mile ahead, cross another floating bridge. Once across, run right on a wide, gravel path and in a few hundred yards reach the Montlake Cut. Follow the trail—now called the Lake Washington Ship Canal Waterside Trail—along the cut to the Montlake Bridge. Just before the bridge, run down some steps and go left at a sidewalk under the bridge. The trail returns to gravel in a few hundred yards.

At **1.4** miles, turn around at West Montlake Park, an open grassy area, and return the way you came.

Nearest Support

The visitor center offers rest rooms and water. Washington Park Arboretum information, 206/543-8800 or www.depts.washington.edu/wpa. Seattle offers many food, drink, and accommodations possibilities.

27 Mercer Slough Nature Park

PAIN 🏃
GAIN ▲▲

Distance	2.6-mile loop
Elevation gain	90 feet
Time	20 to 40 minutes
The route	Flat, gentle run on wide dirt path and boardwalk. Well-signed.
Runnability	100 percent
Season	Year-round
Other users	Hikers
Map	Mercer Slough Nature Park (available at Winters House Visitor Center)

Warm-up

What this urban route lacks in hills and thrills, it makes up for with its variety. Run through marsh and watch crows harass red-tailed hawks and bald eagles overhead; be serenaded by all-frog choruses on lily pad flotillas on Mercer Slough; pass massive red cedars while bouncing your way along the springiest of running surfaces. This is a fun run not far from Interstate 90.

Approach

Take Interstate 90 to exit 9. Head north on Bellevue Way SE for about 0.2 mile and take a right at the South Bellevue Park & Ride. Elevation: 30 feet.

Go

From the southeast corner of the parking lot, find the trailhead and signpost just beyond. Take a left on the wide, gravel path, following directions for Bellefields Trails. Soon, find yourself on a winding boardwalk through a marsh replete with cattails and red-winged blackbirds. At **0.4** mile, go straight through a four-way intersection (remember this spot, you'll be back) and cross Mercer Slough via a bridge. Check the skies for raptors, the slough for buffle-heads and other duckies.

A few hundred yards ahead, take a right at a T-intersection, again following the sign for Bellefields Loop. Bounce along the loop's 0.8-mile springy wood chip and dirt surface while admiring the wetland park's impressive array of

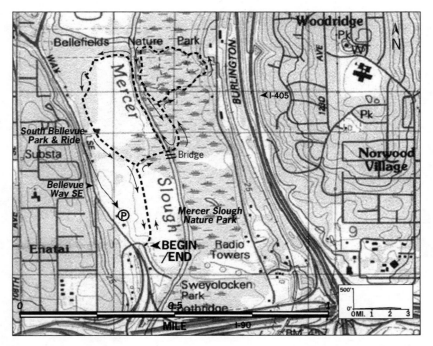

flora and fauna. After running slough-side for a short stretch, complete the loop and take a right back onto the boardwalk from whence you came. Recross the slough bridge (no need to slow down) and this time take a right, following the sign for the Winters House Visitor Center.

Run along the wide wood chip and boardwalk path for about 0.5 mile to the visitor center at **2.0** miles. Pass behind the center. About 150 yards ahead, bear left behind some blueberry farm buildings. Take a right just ahead as you rejoin the boardwalk marsh route you ran earlier. Reach the parking lot at **2.6** miles.

Nearest Support

The Winters House Visitor Center, about 0.25 mile north of the South Bellevue Park & Ride, offers rest rooms, water, and telephones. Park information, 425/452-2752 or www.ci.bellevue.wa.us/parks/majorparks/mercer.htm. The park is located in Bellevue, which offers plenty in the food, drink, and accommodations departments.

28	**I-90 / SNOQUALMIE PASS**
	Wilderness Peak Loop
	PAIN 🏃🏃
	GAIN ▲▲

Distance	4-mile lollipop loop
Elevation gain	1,200 feet
Time	35 minutes to 1 hour
The route	Single track with steady climbing. Wood bridges, big boulders, and fast downhill. Well-signed.
Runnability	90 percent
Season	Year-round
Other users	Hikers
Map	Green Trails Cougar Mountain–Squak Mountain 203S

Warm-up

I once ran this route on the same April Saturday I ran West Tiger No. 3 on Tiger Mountain, less than 5 miles away. While that trail was crawling with humans and their canines, I came across only two people on this route. This loop offers a substantial workout and wilderness experience in a short time and distance. If you're feeling good, do a couple of loops. You also get to sign the summit register at Cougar Mountain's highest point.

Approach

From Interstate 90, take exit 15 and head south on Highway 900. The somewhat discreetly signed Wilderness Creek trailhead is 3 miles down the road on the right. Elevation: 395 feet.

Go

After giving the parking lot map kiosk a once over, head up the obvious Wilderness Creek Trail. Cross said creek about 100 yards ahead, just past a box offering free maps. (Thank you.) Climb steadily on winding single track while gaining a sense of why this is considered the wilderness side of Cougar Mountain. Much of this area has never been logged, lending the forest a primeval feel.

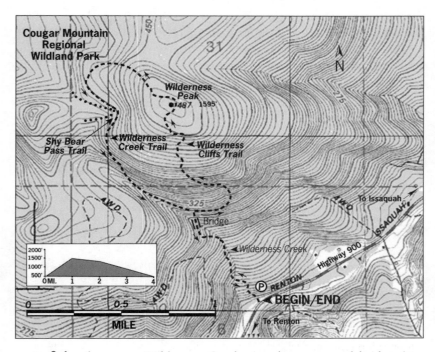

At **0.6** mile, recross Wilderness Creek via a bouncy wood bridge. At a signed T just beyond, run right, following the sign for Big View and Wilderness Peak. When the trail forks at **0.9** mile, go left.

Continue climbing for almost a mile with rocks and roots making the trail a little more technical. At **1.8** miles, arrive at a T and a sign facing away from you. Run right and reach Wilderness Peak's forested summit (1,595 feet) in about 150 yards at **1.9** miles. You'll know it's the summit, not by the grand views (there are none) but by the summit register that invites your comments. ("Because it's there" is always a good one.)

Continue the loop by returning to the sign you just passed and follow its arrow for Shy Bear Pass. Now that you're on the downhill side of things, it's cruising time. At **2.4** miles arrive at a busy intersection where it appears that four trails meet within about 20 yards of each other. Ignore the first right and continue straight ahead to the signed Wilderness Creek Trail. Run left. The trail climbs momentarily, then descends in earnest. Thankfully, it's dusted with forest debris—needles, dirt, leaves, and the like—and offers a nice soft landing. At about **2.7** miles, bound across a boardwalk through a marshy—and in spring, skunk-cabbage stinky—section of trail that goes past huge boulders that appear to be wearing ill-fitting toupees of sword ferns and moss.

You've licked the lollipop when, at **3.4** miles, you reach the Wilderness Peak intersection where you took a right before. From here, it's a quick 0.6 mile back to the parking lot.

Nearest Support

A portable toilet is the only trailhead support. Cougar Mountain Regional Wildland Park information, 206/296-4232 or www.metrokc.gov/parks/rentals/pommar99.htm. For food, drinks, and sleeps, head to Issaquah about 5 miles away off I-90, exit 17.

29 Cougar Mountain Ring

PAIN 🏃🏃

GAIN ▲▲▲

Distance	9-mile loop
Elevation gain	1,400 feet
Time	1.25 to 2.25 hours
The route	Single track and wide, well-maintained trail through forest. Well-signed.
Alternate route	13-mile loop that adds about 1,200 feet of elevation gain.
Runnability	100 percent
Season	Year-round
Other users	Hikers, equestrians
Maps	Green Trails Cougar Mountain–Squak Mountain 203S

Warm-up

This loop is great if you're looking for some distance but you aren't in the mood for killer hills. The route's winding but not-too-technical single track keeps you on your toes and offers lots of fun. The only thing missing are great views, but the peaceful fir and alder forest makes up for it.

Wood bridge on Cougar Mountain Ring t

Approach

From Interstate 90, take exit 13. Head south on Lakemont Boulevard SE for 3.2 miles to the Cougar Mountain parking lot on your left. Elevation: 640 feet.

Go

From the parking lot, head up a dirt road and follow the sign for the Red Town Trail. After about 0.25 mile, turn left on the Cave Hole Trail, a wide, smooth path. When the trail levels out at about 1,100 feet, the most strenuous climbing of the day—not really all that strenuous—is behind you.

At **1.3** miles, bear to the left, continuing to follow the sign for Cave Hole Trail. In about 100 yards cross Clay Pit Road and pick up Coyote Creek Trail on the other side. The single track winds and weaves through forest, offering a fun run without tripping you up with too many obstacles. At **2.1** miles, take a right at the sign for the Klondike Swamp Trail and quickly drop down into said swamp. In about 150 yards, keep your eyes open for Lost Beagle Trail. When you find Lost Beagle, take a left back into the forest, ascending for a not-too-painful 0.5 mile.

At **2.8** miles, continue straight at an intersection and watch as the trail you're on magically transforms itself into the Anti-Aircraft Ridge Trail. Next up, take a right on Cougar Pass Trail at **3.5** miles. A few hundred yards farther, come to the Klondike Swamp Trail again and this time take a left. In 0.25 mile, re-greet Clay Pit Road and, as you did before, cross over the road and pick up a forested trail on the other side. This one is Fred's Railroad Trail. (The sign is about 100 feet into the woods.) At an intersection in 0.5 mile, continue straight. In about 150 yards, run left, following the sign for Shy Bear Pass.

At **4.9** miles, arrive at the pass and take a right, following the sign for the Long View Peak Trail. Ignore the Wilderness Creek Trail just ahead on your left. At **5.3** miles, turn right on the Deceiver Trail. (The short trail to the left leads to the Long View Peak viewpoint, but trees obscure the view quite a bit. Still, it's a nice, open, level area and a great place for food or drink.) About 0.5 mile farther, cross a wood bridge installed in a downed log in stiller-than-still Shy Bear Marsh. (*Note:* Throughout this section of the route, the preponderance of downed logs ratchets up the technical aspect a tad.)

Bear to the right at the Doughty Falls turnoff. At **6.6** miles, run left at the intersection with the Shy Bear Trail. A little less than 0.5 mile farther, hang a ` ignoring the sign for Far Country Lookout. (Once again, trees have · obscured the view.) Take another left just ahead, following the sign for ` Town trailhead. A fast stretch of downhill switchbacking follows.

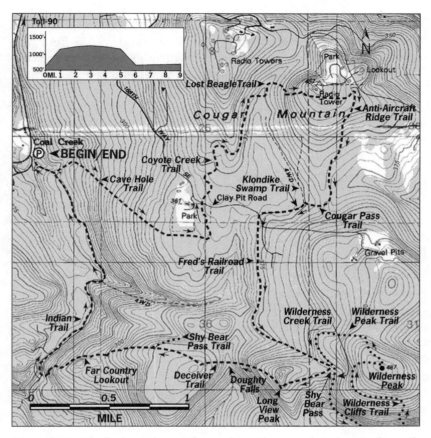

About 0.25 mile farther, take a right on the wide, smooth Indian Trail, a path that some believe dates back more than 8,000 years. From here, it's relatively flat and fun back to the parking lot. At the few intersections along the way, always follow signs for the Red Town trailhead.

Alternate Route

This route can be combined with the Wilderness Peak Trail for a 13-mile route boasting about 2,600 feet of elevation gain. Start at the Wilderness Creek trailhead and follow directions for the Wilderness Peak Loop (see Run #28) to Shy Bear Pass. Instead of taking a left on the Wilderness Creek Trail, continue straight and follow directions for the Cougar Mountain Loop. Once you've made it back to Shy Bear Pass, return to the Wilderness Creek trailhead using the Wilderness Peak Loop description.

Nearest Support

There is no trailhead support. Cougar Mountain Regional Wildland Park information, 206/296-4232 or www.metrokc.gov/parks/rentals/pom-mar99.htm. For food, drinks, and sleeps, head to Issaquah or Bellevue, both less than 5 miles away off I-5.

30

Squak Mountain Loop

PAIN 🏃 🏃 🏃

GAIN ▲ ▲ ▲

Distance	6.7-mile lollipop loop
Elevation gain	1,900 feet
Time	1 to 1.75 hours
The route	Technical single track featuring steep climbs and descents to wide gentle trails. Some signs.
Runnability	90 percent
Season	Year-round
Other users	Hikers
Maps	Green Trails Cougar Mountain–Squak Mountain 203S

Warm-up

Don't veg out on this one. While many of this route's trails are signed in the Tiger/Cougar Mountain manner, others aren't. Even with a map, I've found myself off course more than once. The multiple ups and downs and many fallen logs make this a fun all-around mind/body workout with an added plus: no crowds. Squak is the least visited of the Issaquah Alps (Tiger/Cougar/ Squak Mountains).

Approach

From Interstate 90, take exit 15 and head south on Highway 900. The obscure pullout is about 2.5 miles down the road on the left. You'll know it by the Squak Mountain: West Access Trail sign at the end of the 40-foot pullout that has room for about four cars. Or park about 0.5 mile down the road at the Cougar Mountain Wilderness Creek trailhead and run the road to the start (see Run #29). Elevation: 430 feet.

Go

From the trail sign, ascend to the left up an overgrown dirt road. In a few hundred yards, pass beyond a gate as the route enters a forest and becomes a true trail. It also keeps climbing. At about 1.0 mile, after climbing ~~~~~ 700 feet, take a right on the Chybinski Trail.

Except for a brief descent for a creek crossing, continue climbing fairly steadily for another mile. Not long after the trail finally levels off a bit, look for an unsigned trail spur to the left that leads about 20 yards to the Block House. Take a beverage break and check out this windowless cement structure that will never be featured in *Better Homes and Gardens*. Back on the trail, continue ahead for about 0.25 mile to an unsigned intersection.

Run right, and when you're immediately given the choice between two more trails in a dense thicket of trees, pick the less obvious one straight ahead—the one that starts climbing. About 30 yards in, see the West Peak Trail sign nailed to a tree. Here the fun really begins as this technical, somewhat overgrown stretch of trail travels under and over a scattering of downed logs. If the sword ferns were real swords, they'd be slicing your shins to bits about now. That thing called walking, also known as hiking, will seem like a good idea. Like a pesky dog that keeps following you and won't go home, an odd transmission cable runs along the ground, so look for the cable if you ever wonder if you've gotten off the trail. (It was there in spring 2000.)

At **2.6** miles, after a couple of steep and slippery—but loads of fun—camel humps, reach the summit of Squak's West Peak. You'll know it by the odd structure sporting a partially collapsed roof and the tangle of cables strewn about. Drop quickly on the other side of the structure, then up and down a smaller bump for about 0.25 mile to an unsigned T. Run left and in about 30 feet turn right on the wide Bullitt Fireplace Trail. Climb steeply for a few hundred yards to the said fireplace on your right. It's what's left of the summer home of the Bullitt family, who gave this land to Washington State Parks.

Just past the fireplace, bear left on the obvious trail and drop about a hundred feet over the next 0.3 mile until you reach the signed intersection with the Central Peak Trail. Run right and in another 0.3 mile, **3.8** miles total, reach the summit of Squak Mountain's Central Peak and its accompanying microwave towers. Let out a "Squak!" for good measure.

Head around the fenced-off area. In the northeast corner find the signed Old Griz Trail. Tumble for about 0.25 mile down a steep, technical section in which the trail is at times hard to follow. Bear left at an unsigned intersection (quite a few of those on this route). Tumble some more, and at about **4.3** miles, proceed left at the signed T-intersection with Phil's Trail.

Over the next 0.3 mile, drop almost 400 feet before being dumped onto the wide East Side Trail. It's your ride home. The remaining 2-plus miles are a fun downhill or flat cruise to the parking lot, save for one key intersection. At **5.4** miles, run left at the signed intersection with the Bullitt Access Trail (follow

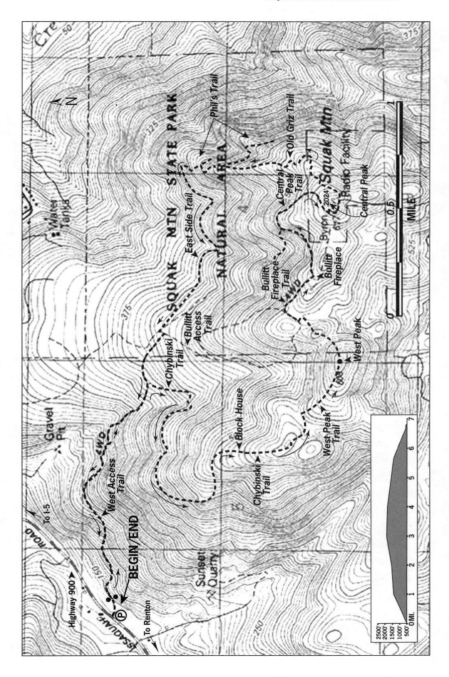

the sign for the fireplace). About 100 yards farther, turn right following the sign for the West Access Trail and head down. Pass the Chybinski Trail in about 0.3 mile and run back the way you came.

Nearest Support

There is no trailhead support. For Squak Mountain State Park information, call Washington State Parks, 800/233-0321. For food, drinks, and sleeps, head to Issaquah about 5 miles away off I-90, exits 17 and 18.

31

I-90 / SNOQUALMIE PASS
West Tiger 3
PAIN 🏃🏃🏃
GAIN ▲▲▲

Distance	5 miles out and back
Elevation gain	2,000 feet
Time	45 minutes to 1.25 hours
The route	Single track and old logging road. Fairly relentless uphill. Views. Signs.
Runnability	80 percent
Season	Year-round
Other users	Hikers
Map	Green Trails Tiger Mountain 204S

Warm-up

This popular and easy-to-follow trail offers a good introduction to trail running on Tiger Mountain. It's steep but not too long, and clear days reward runners with awesome views of Mount Rainier and Puget Sound. West Tiger 3 is also crowded as heck on weekends, not only by humans, but also by their dogs.

A cloudy day atop West Tiger 3

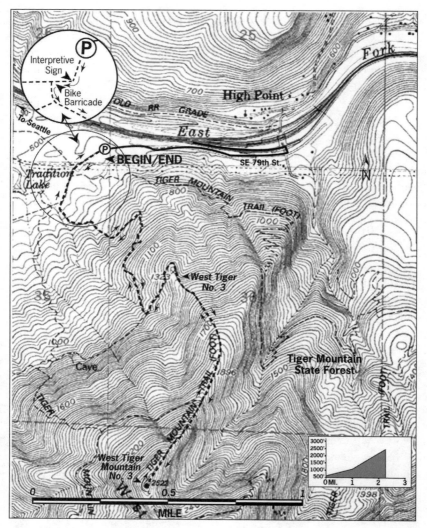

Approach

From Interstate 90, take exit 20. Head south on 270th Avenue SE and take a quick right on SE 79th Street. (Follow the sign for Lake Tradition.) Continue 0.8 mile to the West Tiger Mountain and Tradition Plateau trailhead, also known as the High Point parking lot. Elevation: 520 feet. If this parking lot is full or gated, park at the lower parking lot that you passed at 0.3 mile on your way in.

Go

From the kiosk at the southwest end of the parking lot, follow the sign for trails. In 25 yards, take a right at an interpretive sign. In another 25 yards, run left. Pass through a bike barricade. In about a hundred yards, bear to the left at a fork and follow the sign for West Tiger 3.

Ascend a former logging road that narrows gradually and ignore the gated, yet oddly unsigned trail a few hundred yards ahead on the left. That's the 16-mile Tiger Mountain Trail (TMT).

Continue climbing. At about **0.8** mile, take a left at a T and follow the sign for Tiger Mountain Vista. At **1.3** miles, after a couple of scream-for-mommy steep sections, the trail lets up a little. Catch your breath for the final push to the summit. If it's the weekend, take a moment to see if you can remember the names of all the dogs that have pawed and sniffed you today.

At **2.0** miles, cross an old railroad grade and relish the fact that the summit is only about 0.5 mile away—and about 500 feet of elevation. Suck it up through the final switchbacks. Though you're probably walking at this point, save your food and drink for the summit. Once you glimpse the views, you'll need to do something to keep your jaw from involuntarily hitting the ground.

On the final few hundred yards, several trails seem to lead side by side through the trees to the top. Pick the one that feels most comfortable. At **2.5** miles, reach the open summit of West Tiger 3. Eat, drink, enjoy the Cascade–Puget Sound–Olympic views and think about how fast your descent's going to be. Return the way you came.

Nearest Support

Pit toilets and telephones are available at the West Tiger Mountain and Tradition Plateau trailhead. Information, Issaquah Alps Trails Club, 206/328-0480 or www.issaquahalps.org. Issaquah, which offers plenty in the food, gas, lodging, and more departments, is about 2 miles away off I-5, exit 18.

32 I-90 / SNOQUALMIE PASS
West Tiger Three-Summit Loop

PAIN 🏃🏃🏃🏃

GAIN ▲▲▲

Distance	10.5-mile loop
Elevation gain	3,150 feet
Time	1.5 to 2.5 hours
The route	Technical single track to dirt road. Forest steeps and downhill cruisers. Mountain and city views. Well-signed.
Runnability	80 percent
Season	Year-round
Other users	Hikers, equestrians (Poo Poo Point Trail only)
Map	Green Trails Tiger Mountain 204S

Warm-up

This route takes you to all three of West Tiger Mountain's summits. For laughs, it also throws in the Section Line Trail, which gains more than 1,300 feet in less than a mile. On clear days, views from the summits are spectacular and the 2-plus-mile cruise down Poo Poo Point Trail is always fun. And fun to say. There's a lot to appreciate here.

Approach

From Interstate 90, take exit 20. Head south on 270th Avenue SE and take a quick right on SE 79th Street. (Follow the sign for Lake Tradition.) Continue 0.8 mile to the West Tiger Mountain and Tradition Plateau trailhead, also known as the High Point parking lot. Elevation: 520 feet. If this parking lot is full or gated, park at the lower parking lot that you passed at 0.3 mile on your way in.

Go

From the kiosk at the southwest end of the parking lot, follow the sign for trails. In 25 yards, turn right at an interpretive sign. In another 25 yards, run left. After passing through a bike barricade, follow the sign for the Bus Trail. After 100 yards, take a right at another sign for the Bus Trail. Another 150 yards along a pleasant narrow path gets you to the Nook Trail, and the last of your early-run turns. Run left. Begin climbing steadily on a wide trail that gradually narrows and becomes more technical.

Dense forest on the Bypass Trail

At 1.2 miles, run right at the sign for the Section Line Trail. Traverse a hill for about 0.25 mile on a narrow level trail. Relish this level running. It'll be your last for awhile. Turn left at the next intersection and start climbing— really climbing. The narrow, winding Section Line Trail climbs more than 1,300 feet in less than a mile, entering deeper, darker, denser forest the higher you go.

After about 0.5 mile and an 800-feet-plus elevation gain, cross the West Tiger Railroad Grade Trail and keep on keepin' on. At 2.4 miles, pop out of the forest and onto the West Tiger No. 3 Trail. Turn right and in 50 yards the first summit (2,522 feet) is yours. On clear days, the views are amazing, so soak them in while you replenish yourself with food and drink.

Head straight across the bare summit area in the direction of West Tiger No. 2 (the close hill to the southeast wearing the telecommunications tower crown) and find a trail that switchbacks down into the forest. After about 0.25 mile of downhill running, begin the short ascent to your second summit, passing through the Tiger Mountain Trail intersection on the way. At 2.9 miles, emerge from the forest at the summit and just below the giant tower (2,757 feet).

Two summits down, one to go.

Find the dirt road to the right and drop about 200 feet over the next 0.25 mile until you reach a gate. Just beyond the gate, take the left fork, a dirt road that climbs steeply to the summit of West Tiger No. 3. At 3.2 miles, take a left

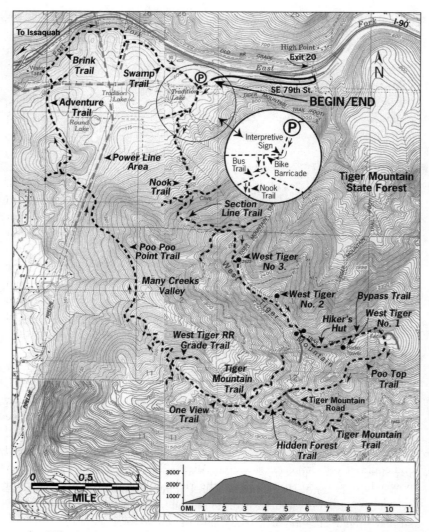

at the Hiker's Hut onto the Bypass Trail, which, not surprisingly, bypasses the summit. (Signs here seem to infer that the towers will fry your brains and other parts, so you're not allowed near the actual top. You're close enough, however, to give yourself credit for a summit (2,948 feet).

The Bypass Trail drops into a seemingly pitch-black forest, so on bright days be aware that it will take a few moments for your eyes to adjust. Traverse the side of a hill on a narrow trail that offers a landing so soft you'll never want to leave it.

After about 0.25 mile, run right at a somewhat confusing sign. You're looking for the Poo Top Trail. Climb steeply out of the forest and pop out on the other side of the tower and the ominous-looking buildings associated with it. Find an unmarked, somewhat obscure trail on the other side of a dirt road, and upon reentering the forest, descend rather rapidly. This is the Poo Top Trail (no laughing, please). Because it's not nearly as easy to follow as what you've been running to this point, take it slow. The trail slaloms through dense forest for about 0.75 mile, finally emerging at a bend in Tiger Mountain Road (dirt) at **4.4** miles.

With the most arduous climbing and descending behind you, take advantage of this level ground for some eats and drinks. Cross the road and pick up the Hidden Forest Trail by following the sign for the Tiger Mountain Trail. After about 0.25 mile, turn right on Tiger Mountain Trail. A few hundred yards farther, turn left at the sign for the One View Trail. The bad news is that trees now obscure the one view. The good news is that, except for one minor ascent, the next 3-plus miles are all flat or downhill.

At **5.2** miles, go straight and continue descending through a four-way intersection with the West Tiger Railroad Grade Trail. Though there's no sign that says so, you're now on the Poo Poo Point Trail. Ahem. (Actually, it's a term from Tiger Mountain's logging days.) After a fast descent down a multitude of switchbacks and a slower, gentler traverse across Many Creeks Valley, exit the forest at **8.0** miles and enter an open power-line area.

Just ahead and to the left, follow a sign for the Adventure Trail. Reenter the woods. In about 0.25 mile, run right and venture onto the Adventure Trail. The minor climb might seem cruel at this point, but hey, you're a trail runner, you'll deal. Follow for about 0.75 mile and enter another open power-line area, this one a bit overgrown. Continue straight, bearing left at a fork to pick up the Brink Trail. Reach another open power-line area about 0.5 mile ahead and continue on, reentering the forest. After 0.25 mile or so, enter yet another power-line area. This time bear to the right, following a grassy path. Just ahead, below a large tower, take a left on a path that reenters the forest. As the sign says, it's the Swamp Trail and the last trail for this run. Follow to the south end of the parking lot at **10.5** miles.

Nearest Support

Pit toilets and telephones are available at the West Tiger Mountain and Tradition Plateau trailhead. Information, Issaquah Alps Trails Club, 206/328-0480 or www.issaquahalps.org. Issaquah, which offers plenty in the food, gas, lodging, and more departments, is about 2 miles away off I-5, exit 18.

33 | I-90 / SNOQUALMIE PASS
South & Middle Tiger

PAIN 🏃🏃🏃

GAIN ▲ ▲ ▲

Distance	12.3-mile lollipop loop
Elevation gain	2,650 feet
Time	1.5 hours to 2.5 hours
The route	Technical single track and former logging roads through forest. Includes two mini-summits. Some signs.
Runnability	95 percent
Season	Year-round
Other users	Hikers
Map	Green Trails Tiger Mountain 204S

Warm-up

This route is an exploration of Tiger Mountain State Forest's southern region. Unlike routes on Tiger's north side—which is actually West Tiger Mountain—this combination of trails doesn't start out with a killer climb. In fact, despite its 2,600-plus feet of elevation gain, it's almost all very runnable. Watch for nettles of the stinging variety as sections of the trail tend to get overgrown.

Approach

Take Interstate 90 to exit 17 in Issaquah. Drive south through town on Front Street (which eventually becomes Issaquah–Hobart Road) for 8.2 miles. Turn left the *second* time you come to Tiger Mountain Road. The unmarked trailhead is about 0.3 mile farther on the right. There is no parking lot, so park on the opposite side of the road in the wide shoulder. Elevation: 560 feet.

Go

Just up the wooded trail, find the Tiger Mountain Trail (TMT) sign. The 16-mile TMT leads from the south end of Tiger Mountain State Forest to the north, and much of this route follows the TMT. Begin a gentle climb. At **1.0** mile, pass a number "1" nailed to a tree (guess what it refers to). About 0.5 mile farther reach Hobart Gap, a signed T-intersection with an old railroad grade. Take a look around—you'll be returning to this spot.

Run left and then take a quick right up an old logging road that climbs sharply. After rounding a bend, leave the forest temporarily and run across an open, and potentially overgrown, power-line area. At **1.8** miles, reenter the forest, now on the South Tiger Traverse Trail. In about 0.6 mile, come to a technical switchback section, one of this route's few steep segments.

Stump face on South & Middle Tiger

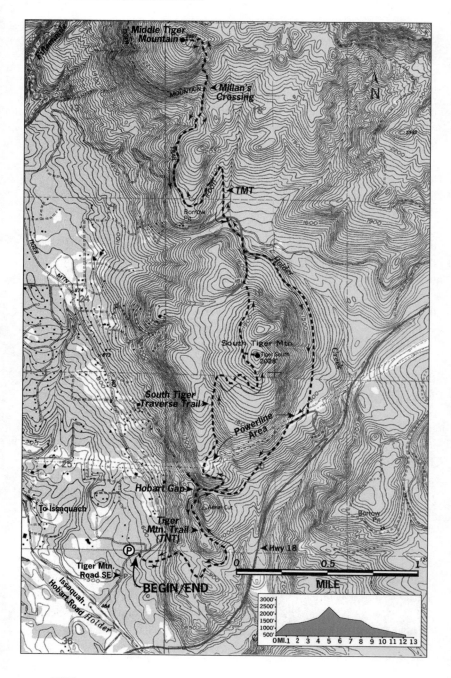

At about **2.5** miles, just after the trail levels out, look for a somewhat obscure trail to the right. Find the large stump also on the right that resembles a face with deep-set eyes looking away from you. The trail, which was cut by Gig Harbor trail-running guru Ron Nicholl, starts right there and leads after about 0.25 mile of log leaping to the summit of South Tiger Mountain (elevation: 2,028 feet). You'll find no views, but there is a summit register to sign.

After the quick up and back to the South Tiger summit, return to the South Tiger Traverse Trail and take a right, continuing north. At **3.4** miles, after a level and even slightly downhill stretch, come to a T-intersection with a logging road at the edge of a clearcut area. Run right on the road and descend for a while until you merge with another dirt road at **3.8** miles. This is actually the TMT again and a spot you'll be returning to, so take a look around.

Bear to the left. At **4.0** miles, come to a T-intersection with yet another dirt road. (Not that it matters, but the TMT, which you're on, is likely gated at this intersection.) Cross to the other side and find a well-marked single-track trail (also the TMT) about 5 yards to the left that leads into dense woods. Climb gradually over the next mile or so and begin climbing in earnest about 0.5 mile after that. At about **5.8** miles, reach Millan's Crossing, a signed four-way intersection and your last breather before the toughest part of the course, the 0.5-mile push to the top of Middle Tiger.

Take a right, following the sign for Middle Tiger Mountain. Climb more than 500 feet on this steep technical stretch, perhaps the only part of this route that you'll walk. The trail here is extra tricky because it's not only narrow but also on a mini-ridge, from which it'd be easy to tumble a few yards. Use caution on the return run.

At **6.3** miles, reach the 2,607-foot steeple of Middle Tiger, with no register and, unfortunately, just a narrow slice of views. Eat, drink, be merry, and prepare yourself for the ride home. Return the way you came until the intersection you reached earlier (at 3.8 miles). This time continue straight, following the sign for Tiger Mountain Trail. The dirt road soon narrows down to a fast, flat, and downhill single track.

At **9.9** miles, come to a T-intersection with a dirt road. Run left across the same power-line area you crossed earlier, this time about 0.75 mile farther east. After 100 yards, run right on a dirt road that follows directly below the power lines. Just before the road starts to climb, turn left on a trail that's likely to be significantly overgrown. Look for the Tiger Mountain Trail sign sticking up out of the weeds about 10 feet in.

In about 100 yards, reenter the woods and bounce along a streambed-like trail, dropping elevation quickly. At **10.8** miles, return to Hobart Gap. This time take a left and return the way you came to the TMT trailhead at **12.3** miles, where you started.

Nearest Support

There is no trailhead support. Information, Issaquah Alps Trails Club, 206/328-0480 or www.issaquahalps.org. Issaquah, which offers plenty in the food, gas, lodging, and more departments, is about 8 miles away off Issaquah–Hobart Road.

34 Tiger Mountain 6/12 Summits

PAIN 🏃🏃🏃🏃🏃
GAIN ▲▲▲▲

Distance	17 miles point to point
Elevation gain	4,800 feet
Time	3 to 4.5 hours
The route	Technical single track to dirt road. Forest steeps and downhill cruisers. Views. Some signs.
Alternate route	34-miles out-and-back
Runnability	80 percent
Season	Year-round
Other users	Hikers, mountain bikers (on one short stretch)
Map	Green Trails Tiger Mountain 204S

Warm-up

In 1974, the Stylistics had a rhythm and blues hit, "Let's Put It All Together." That's what we do with this route that includes visits to each of Tiger Mountain State Forest's six summits. It combines parts of Run #32, West Tiger

Looking up the steep Section Line Trail

Three-Summit Loop, and Run #33, South & Middle Tiger, along with a middle section that appears in this write-up only. Many ultrarunners train by making this an out-and-back run, thus doubling the pain and gain thus the "12" in Tiger 6/12. I send a shout out to Gig Harbor ultrarunner and writer Ron Nicholl for putting this route together.

Approach

This route requires two cars. Park one car at the Tiger Mountain Trail south trailhead on Tiger Mountain Road, the approach for Run #33, South & Middle Tiger. Park the other vehicle at the High Point trailhead as described in the approach for Run #32, West Tiger Three-Summit Loop, which is where you start. Elevation: 520 feet.

Go

(We join this route description already in progress . . .) See Run #32, West Tiger Three-Summit Loop, and follow it to the Bypass Trail just past the Hiker's Hut on West Tiger 1. At **3.5** miles, at the signed intersection with a trail that leads to the right and up to the Poo Top Trail, continue straight, following the sign for the Bootleg Trail. Traverse the north flank of the mountain for about 0.6 mile to an unsigned, easy-to-miss T-intersection. Take a left and start descending immediately. (When I ran this trail in summer 2000, green ribbons were tied to the bushes at this key intersection and orange dots were sprayed on certain trees lining the descent.)

At **5.0** miles, run right at an unmarked fork and continue dropping through an increasingly overgrown area. (In summer 2000, a small tree was decorated with Christmas ornaments to mark which way to go.) Pass another obscure trail on the left. Shortly after the route mostly levels off, turn left on the unsigned East Tiger Trail.

Wind your way through dense, seldom-visited forest, dropping some and climbing some. At **7.3** miles, after a particularly steep stretch, come to the intersection with the Prescott Railroad Grade Trail. Cross the Prescott and find the faint continuation of the East Tiger Trail about 20 feet to your left. This section of trail is obscure with a capital O, so go slow at first, making sure not to lose it. It's also steep, gaining about 500 feet in 0.5 mile with many downed logs that make it an adventurous climb (and an adventurous descent too, since you'll be returning on this same stretch).

Shortly after the trail levels off, take a right onto a dirt road and continue climbing. At **8.1** miles, reach the top of East Tiger Mountain, at 3,004 feet the

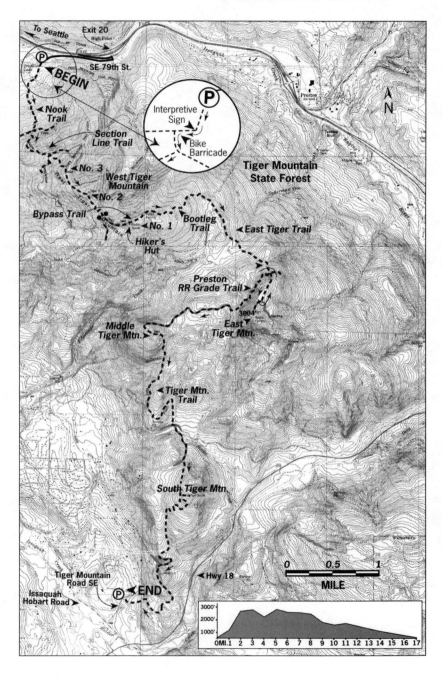

highest point in the park and your fourth summit so far. Enjoy more great views, replenish yourself some more, and head back down, following the way you came, as far as the Prescott Railroad Grade Trail. Run left on this wide, mostly level—though at times root-studded—trail. Mountain bikes are allowed here, so keep your eyes and ears open.

At **9.6** miles, run right at a T-intersection with a dirt road. Head due west, losing some elevation before an intersection to the right with another dirt road a little more than 0.5 mile ahead. Continue straight around a gate. After rounding a bend, start climbing somewhat steeply. Upon reentering the forest, the road abruptly ends. Find the Middle Tiger Trail climbing steeply into the forest on the left. Just ahead, up the steep 0.25-mile stretch of trail, reach the summit of Middle Tiger Mountain at **11.0** miles (elevation: 2,607 feet).

From here, see Run #33, South & Middle Tiger, and follow that route description from the 6.3-mile mark—the top of Middle Tiger Mountain—to the end at the Tiger Mountain Trail trailhead on Tiger Mountain Road SE.

Alternate Route

To run this as the 34-mile out-and-back route, simply turn around at the Tiger Mountain Road SE trailhead and return back to the High Point parking area the way you came. If it's just the twelve summits you're after, turn around at the summit of South Tiger Mountain and return to High Point for a distance of about 28.5 miles.

Nearest Support

Rest rooms and pit toilets are available at the West Tiger Mountain and Tradition Plateau trailhead, also known as the High Point trailhead. The Tiger Mountain trailhead offers no services. Information, Issaquah Alps Trails Club, 206/328-0480 or www.issaquahalps.org. Issaquah, which offers plenty in the food, gas, lodging, and more departments, is located off I-5, exits 17 and 18.

35 | I-90 / SNOQUALMIE PASS
Mount Si

PAIN 🏃🏃🏃🏃🏃

GAIN ▲▲▲▲

Distance	8.5 miles out and back
Elevation gain	3,400 feet
Time	1.5 to 2.5 hours
The route	Mostly wide rock- and root-strewn trail that climbs relentlessly. Views. Signs.
Runnability	80 percent
Season	April to November; lower elevations year-round
Other users	Hikers
Maps	Mount Si NRCA and Upper Snoqualmie Valley Trail Systems (DNR)

Warm-up

Hey, boys and girls, wanna get in shape for pretty much anything? Run Mount Si. You'll thrill as you gain about 800 feet over each mile of this way popular trail, a pain fave of many Seattle trail runners. If you're an experienced rock climber, consider scrambling up the Haystack, a 200-foot rock outcrop

Running high on Mount Si

that rewards with 360-degree views of seemingly every square inch of Washington State. (*Note:* Because it tops out at 4,167 feet, Mount Si's upper reaches often are snow covered through the spring.)

Approach

Take Interstate 90 to exit 32 in North Bend. Drive north on 436th Avenue for about 0.5 mile to North Bend Way. Turn left and in about 0.3 mile, turn right on Mount Si Road. The well-signed trailhead parking lot is 2.4 miles ahead on the left. Elevation: 670 feet.

Go

After browsing through the found items on display near the trailhead kiosk — How *does* one lose a pair of shorts?—find the obvious trail. Run this tame prelude for about 50 yards to where the real Mount Si Trail—and the real climbing—begins. Rock- and root-riddled pretty much all the way to the top, the densely wooded, relentlessly uphill trail is nonetheless easy to follow. Mileage markers at half-mile intervals allow you to gauge your progress—or lack thereof—on the way up.

Just past **1.0** mile, views open up to the left (south) and if it's clear, they include a nice picture-window view of Mount Rainier. At about **1.8** miles, you'll reach Snagg Flats, a 100-yard level stretch that, given all the climbing you've done to this point, will have you feeling like you're running downhill. It's a great place to chug from the water jug. Take a few moments to marvel at some massive fire-scorched firs that over the centuries have survived multiple conflagrations.

Then, climb, climb, climb, climb, climb. Count the number of individuals you come across training for Rainier ascents, obvious by their huge packs, ice axes, and plastic boots. The higher you go, the rockier the trail, something to be aware of on what is sure to be a screaming descent.

At **3.5** miles, the forest opens up once again to the south, revealing even more impressive mountain views. Stop and gawk or, if you can, wait 0.5 mile for the top. At **4.0** miles, you reach Haystack Basin, a talus-strewn shoulder that amazes with 180-degree views guaranteed to knock your Ultimax socks off. It's a great place to eat, drink, and kick back, as the kids say.

Scramble up the rocks and boulders to gain views west toward Seattle, Puget Sound, and the Olympics. Above, check out the Haystack, Mount Si's few-hundred-feet-high rocky peak, which appears daunting but is not quite so scary from its east flank. For a closer look, or if you're experienced in rock climbing

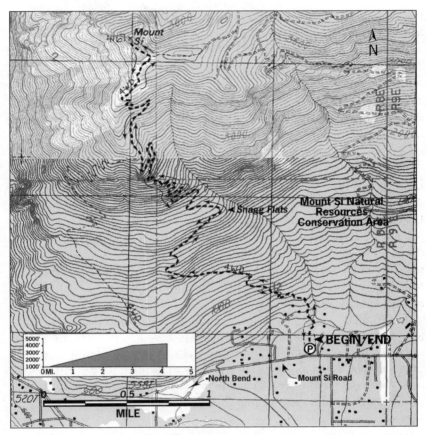

and intend to scramble to the top, follow the trail a few hundred yards east. The 360-degree views from the roof might prompt you to yell "I'm the king of the world!" à la Leonardo DiCaprio, but it's probably better if you don't.

Return the way you came, but fasten your seatbelts. It's likely to be a bumpy ride.

Nearest Support

The Mount Si trailhead offers water and rest rooms. Mount Si Natural Resources Conservation Area information, 360/825-1631. North Bend, which offers plenty in the food, drink, and lodging departments, is about 3 miles away on North Bend Way.

36 Rattlesnake Mountain

PAIN 🏃🏃🏃

GAIN ▲ ▲ ▲

Distance	7 miles out and back
Elevation gain	2,600 feet
Time	1 to 1.75 hours
The route	Technical single track and old logging road through forest and along ridge. Views. Few signs.
Alternate route	11-mile point-to-point route from Rattlesnake Lake to Snoqualmie Winery.
Runnability	90 percent
Season	Year-round, though in winter, higher elevations likely to be snow-covered
Other users	Hikers
Map	USGS North Bend (7.5' series)

Warm-up

Looking south from Mount Si, Rattlesnake Mountain is the ridge that appears to have better seats than Si for Mount Rainier viewing. Parts of this route are intestine-like and prone to overgrowth—not to mention steep—so don't plan on setting any speed records, either up or down. The views will also slow you down—they're spectacular en route as well as from the summit.

Approach

From Interstate 90, take exit 32 in North Bend. Head south on 436th Avenue SE (which turns into Cedar Falls Road SE) for 2.7 miles and park at the signed parking lot to the right. Elevation: 920 feet.

Go

From the parking lot, follow signs for the Rattlesnake Ledge Trail. (Rattlesnake Ledge is an impressive viewpoint along the way.) Pass around a gate and run a gravel road that follows the shoreline of Rattlesnake Lake for about 0.25 mile. At **0.3** mile, just after a couple of portable toilets, find a map kiosk and proper trail, which heads steeply up into the dense forest. Leave the flatlands behind and go for the gusto, my friend.

Just ahead, run through a four-way intersection and continue climbing. Like many northwest Washington trails, Rattlesnake Mountain is full of exposed roots assuming the role of mini-hurdles and making an already technical trail seem even more so. While there's evidence of burly folk who've cut many of the switchbacks, don't take the trail less taken, but rather take the trail most traveled.

At **1.5** miles, after gaining about 1,100 feet, you'll reach a narrow ridge and a sign for Rattlesnake Ledge and some other trails. Take a left following the arrow for the Rattlesnake Mountain Trail. (Consider visiting the ledge with its views aplenty—only 100 yards away—on the way down when you'll be more inclined to dawdle and gawk.)

Mount Rainier from Rattlesnake Mountain

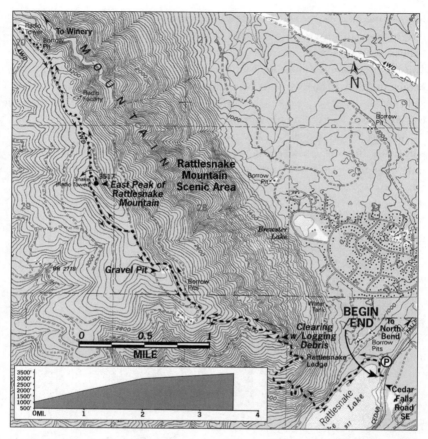

Continue climbing along a narrow ridge with views opening up north from time to time toward North Bend and the Snoqualmie Valley. Be on the watch for mini-trails that look like the main route but are only spurs leading to ridge lookout points. At about **2.0** miles, the trail narrows. When brush is overgrown, this makes for some knock-kneed running. Consider low-cut gaiters to keep your shoes free of debris.

About 0.3 mile farther, reach a logging debris-riddled clearing that's actually a great place to stop, drink, eat, and admire views that are getting better and better the higher you go. To the south, Rainier appears to be growing, and behind you the mountains of the Alpine Lakes region are demanding a once-over. If you've brought a camera, snap away.

Once it's time to carry on, run to the left. After about 50 feet of brush and small trees, reach another clearing. This time, run right, traverse a small dirt hill, and continue into the woods on your winding, narrow, knock-kneed way. Given the trail's roots, rocks, downed logs, and limbs, the term "obstacle course" will enter your mind.

At **2.7** miles, run straight across a brief clearing, following the Rattlesnake Mountain Trail (RMT) sign. After a quick jaunt through the forest, take a right on an overgrown road that continues climbing. In a few hundred yards, pass by an old gravel pit on your way up.

At **3.0** miles, run right at an intersection with a logging road. Take a look around because this is a turn you don't want to miss on the way back. In 0.25 mile, take a left on another logging road, which starts out flat but, soon enough, starts climbing and becomes your ride to the top. At **3.5** miles, reach the East Peak of Rattlesnake Mountain, its highest point (elevation: 3,517 feet). You'll know it's the top when you see the towers. Tune in and turn on to groovy 360-degree views of mountains, valleys, towns, and highways galore. Sigh at the beauty of Mount Si, the Olympics, Baker, Rainier—they're all here.

Return the way you came, stopping at Rattlesnake Ledge if so inclined.

Alternate Route

For a roughly 11-mile point-to-point run that spans the entire Rattlesnake Mountain ridge, park one car at the old Snoqualmie Winery off I-90, exit 27, and make this your destination. Run the above described route, but when you reach the top at **3.5** miles, instead of heading back down, follow the network of trails and old roads leading northwest along the ridge spine.

Nearest Support

The Rattlesnake Lake trailhead offers no support, though there is a portable toilet about 0.3 mile into the trail. Department of Natural Resources South Puget Sound Region information, 360/825-1631. North Bend, which offers plenty in the food, drink, and lodging departments, is about 5 miles away on North Bend Way.

37 Snoqualmie Valley Trail

PAIN 🏃🏃

GAIN ▲ ▲

Distance	9.8 miles out and back
Elevation gain	400 feet
Time	1.25 to 2.25 hours
The route	Wide, gravel road along old railroad grade. No signs.
Alternate route	4.9 miles point to point.
Runnability	100 percent
Season	Year-round
Other users	Hikers, bikers, equestrians
Maps	Mount Si NRCA and Upper Snoqualmie Valley Trail Systems (DNR)

Warm-up

Not in the mood for hills but still want a trail-running experience? Run this stretch of the 35-mile Snoqualmie Valley Trail, which offers a mild elevation gain on the way out and a gentle gravity push on the way back. Enjoy Boxley Creek and occasional Mount Si views along the way.

Approach

Head east on Interstate 90 to exit 32 near North Bend. Drive north on 436th Way SE for about 0.5 mile. Turn right on North Bend Way and continue for about 0.7 mile to a gravel parking area on the right side of the road. Park here. The trail is just ahead beyond a gate. Elevation: 520 feet.

Go

Proceed beyond the gate onto the wide gravel road and head south for almost 5 miles. The trail gains a little less than 100 feet per mile—not bad on the way out, and a nice push on the way back.

At **0.3** mile, pass under I-90. About 0.25 mile farther, cross the South Fork of the Snoqualmie River via a bridge. Stop, look, and listen when crossing a residential street at **0.6** mile, but for the most part, put 'er on cruise control all the way to the parking area at Rattlesnake Lake at **4.9** miles. Return on the gentle, slightly downhill trail the way you came.

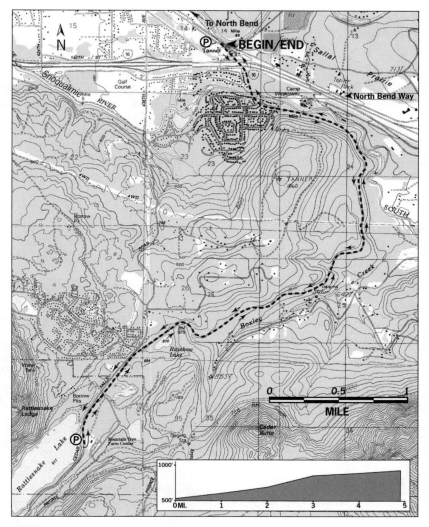

Alternate Route

For a flat and fast one-way trail run, park one car at the North Bend Way parking lot (described above) and the other at the Rattlesnake Lake trailhead, described in Run #36, Rattlesnake Mountain. Start at the Rattlesnake Lake trailhead and run to North Bend Way from there.

Nearest Support

There is no trailhead support. King County Parks Trails information, 206/296-4281 or www.metrokc.gov/parks/trails/trails/snoqv.htm. For food, drink, and accommodations, North Bend is 2 miles west of the trailhead off North Bend Way.

38 Melakwa & Pratt Lakes Loop

PAIN 🏃🏃🏃🏃🏃
GAIN ▲▲▲▲▲

Distance	13.7 miles point to point
Elevation gain	3,350 feet
Time	3 to 5 hours
The route	Wide, easy trail to technical, hard-to-follow single track in alpine wilderness. Views. Signs.
Alternate route	16.7-mile loop
Runnability	75 percent
Season	July to October
Other users	Hikers
Maps	Green Trails Bandera 206; Snoqualmie Pass 207
Permits	Northwest Forest Pass; Alpine Lakes Wilderness Permit (free and available at trailheads)

Warm-up

This wilderness loop is truly a feast for the eyes. You pass plunging waterfalls, pristine alpine lakes, and sky-scratching peaks, not to mention that you run through forests of solitude. While the first part of this route—Denny Creek to

Melakwa Lake

Melakwa Lake—and the last part—Pratt Lake to the Pratt Lake trailhead—are mostly on wide, well-marked trail, the middle stretch is a challenge. Bush-whacking, route finding, and giving it your best mountain goat impression are required. The stunning wilderness experience makes it all worth it.

Approach

From Interstate 90, take exit 47 and head north. About 0.1 mile farther, take a left. The road ends at the Pratt Lake trailhead parking lot, 0.4 mile ahead on both sides of the road, so park the first car here. To get to the Denny Creek trailhead, which is where the route starts, drive back the way you came but continue straight where you took the left 0.4 mile back. About 0.25 mile past that, take a left and follow the unsigned road for about 2.4 miles to just past the Denny Creek Campground. Take a left on a road that soon crosses the Snoqualmie River and follow for about 0.25 mile to the Denny Creek trail-head at the end of the road. Elevation: 2,300 feet.

Go

From the parking lot, begin a gradual climb through forest on a wide, well-maintained trail. At **0.3** mile, cross Denny Creek (not for the last time either) via a narrow bridge. Just across, the trail becomes more rocky and root-strewn. Soon hear, then see, I-90 far overhead above the treetops. It's an odd sensation.

At **1.1** miles, recross Denny Creek, while admiring the wide flat rocks scoured smooth by the water, which is likely to give you a bit of a wet foot. On the other side, the trail starts climbing with meaning. In about 0.5 mile, leave the forest and reach an area where you're suddenly surrounded by tow-ering peaks on all sides. This is Cascades running at its finest, my friends. Soon the trail crosses the first of many rock- and boulder-strewn areas, the kind that eats ankles and knees like yours for breakfast. At about **1.8** miles, stop to gawk at plunging Keekwulee Falls, a few hundred yards to the right.

Over the next 2 miles, the route offers a fairly consistent theme. It's called climbing. Cross open rocky stretches, enter forest, exit forest, cross open rocky stretches, etc.—all while getting farther and farther from the center of the earth. While certainly challenging, super views make the going fun.

At **4.0** miles, reach Hemlock Pass, at 4,600 feet, the highest point on today's run. Almost immediately, drop quickly into the Melakwa Lake Basin. Despite the sharp descent, large rocks and roots resembling gnarled plumbing fixtures will prevent you from exceeding the speed limit. About 0.5 mile farther, just before Melakwa Lake, take a hard left following the sign for Tuscohatchie Lake.

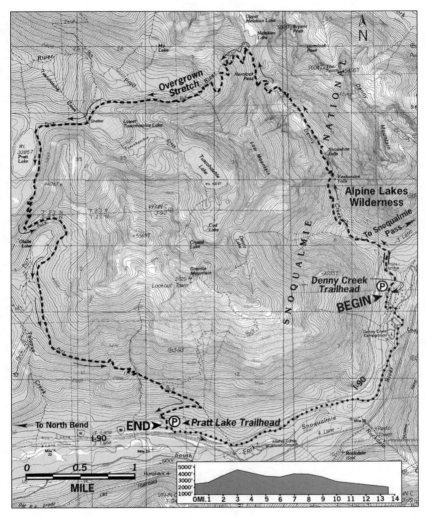

(Before you do, however, check out Melakwa Lake. It's only about 100 yards straight ahead and is a great stop for a drink and an eat. You can toast the fact that two-thirds of the climbing on today's route is behind you.)

Heading toward Tuscohatchie (one of my favorite country 'n' western songs, by the way) the trail drops quickly, offering boulders, rocks, stream crossings, and downed trees galore as obstacles. If, during this downhill stretch, you have trouble following the trail, just listen for a creek and you'll know you're on the right track. After dropping about 800 feet from Melakwa Lake, the route enters a very overgrown stretch of trail. On and off for about 1.5 miles, the going is slow as nettles, salmonberries, and other vegetation do their darndest to cover up the trail area. Adding to the fun is the fact that the trail— which is there, trust me—is rocky and riddled with holes.

At 7.4 miles, reach Lower Tuscohatchie Lake, a pristine mountain lake and a great replenishment stop. Bask in the sun on one of the large rocks lining the shore. Continue along the lake to the southwest side. After crossing a primitive wood bridge, find the trail straight ahead. After a short stretch of forest, sweeping views open up to the right. In little more than 0.5 mile, after yet another boulder field, reach Pratt Lake, the third and final big pond on the route. Run left at the sign for the Pratt Lake trailhead and get crackin' on that final third of today's climbing—about 800 feet—that's still ahead of you.

The serpentine ascent snakes in and out of forest, meadow, and of course boulder fields. At 9.4 miles, the trail levels off in forest. Maps say there's an intersection with a trail here and to bear left. When I ran this, I didn't notice the intersection, so I just stayed on the obvious trail and was fine. Now, with all of today's climbing behind you, begin the descent to the Pratt Lake trailhead. Just ahead, trees open up to the right to reveal regal Mount Rainier peering down majestically on Talapus Lake.

At 10.6 miles, continue straight and down at the intersection with the Talapus Lake Trail, following the Pratt Lake trailhead sign. From here, your descent picks up speed on wide, if at times rock- and root-studded, trail. Several creeks cross the trail, offering a good foot soaking as you return to lower elevations at the rate of about 700 feet per mile. At the intersection with the Granite Mountain Trail, run right and continue descending following the sign for I-90. It's 1.2 miles farther to the Pratt Lake trailhead at 13.7 miles.

Alternate Route

To run this as a 16.7-mile continuous loop, park at the Pratt Lake trailhead and run 3 miles on pavement to the Denny Creek trailhead, following the above driving directions.

Nearest Support

Pit toilets are available at the Pratt Lake and Denny Creek trailheads, but no water or telephones. Camping, rest rooms, and water are available at the Denny Creek Campground. Alpine Lakes Wilderness information, 509/548-6977 or www.fs.fed.us/r6/mbs/wilderness/alakes.htm. Food, drink, and accommodations are available off I-90 in North Bend about 15 miles west.

I-90 / SNOQUALMIE PASS
Kendall Katwalk

PAIN 🏃🏃🏃🏃

GAIN ▲▲▲▲

Distance	11.4 miles out and back
Elevation gain	2,700 feet
Time	1.5 to 2.75 hours
The route	Wide trail to technical single track in alpine wilderness, including boulder fields. Signs. Views.
Alternate routes	Numerous
Runnability	90 percent
Season	July to October
Other users	Hikers
Map	Green Trails Snoqualmie Pass 207
Permits	Northwest Forest Pass; Alpine Lakes Wilderness Permit (free and available at trailhead)

Warm-up

Simply put, Kendall Katwalk offers a super Cascade trail-running experience. Rocky peaks, emerald valleys, fields of wildflowers, all watched over by a looming Mount Rainier—what could be better? Then there's the Katwalk, a narrow stretch of trail blasted into granite and featuring a drop-off that's an acrophobe's

Cruising the Kendall Katwalk

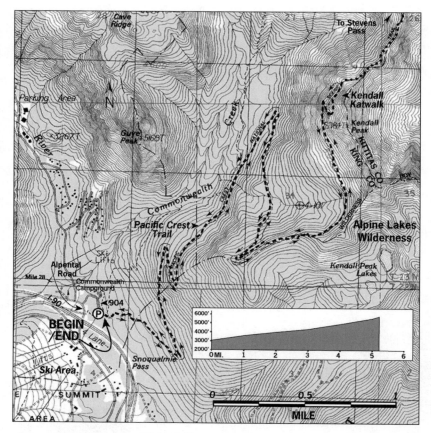

nightmare. Another plus: Though this route gains about 2,700 feet, topping out at about 5,400 feet, much of the climb is gradual enough and interspersed with flat stretches, so running is possible pretty much the whole way.

Approach

From Interstate 90, take exit 52 at Snoqualmie Pass. Head north on Alpental Road. A few hundred yards ahead, turn right at the sign for the Pacific Crest Trail. Just ahead, take another right following the sign for 9041. The parking lot is just ahead. Elevation: 3,000 feet.

Go

After filling out an Alpine Lakes Wilderness Pass, find the obvious trail behind the kiosk and get crackin'. About 100 yards in, turn right at an unmarked

T-intersection. Continue as the trail narrows to single track and offers rocks and roots—as well as some elevation gain—for your enjoyment.

At about **2.0** miles, descend for about 0.25 mile through a technical boulder field that, frankly, has no regard for ankles or knees. That done, reenter forest. About 0.5 mile ahead, run right at a fork, following the sign for the Pacific Crest Trail. Begin climbing steeply. As you pass through a semi-open area, marvel at Red Mountain straight ahead, looking so red it boggles the head.

The trail makes an abrupt 180-degree turn south at **3.0** miles but continues climbing steadily. When trees and avalanche chutes allow, peek at peaks all around: truly inspiring. Cross a couple of creeks that, depending on their flow, are likely to give you a dose of soaked socks. In a little less than a mile, the trail levels off a bit and offers a fun ride on a wide traverse that again heads north.

At about **4.7** miles, emerge from the forest and be dazzled—whether you want to be or not—by the views of mountains and wildflowers that seem to stretch to infinity. Below, check out the freeway and the Snoqualmie ski areas. Ahead, when the trail again swings back toward the south, Rainier's frosty visage appears seemingly at eye level.

Soon the trail becomes a narrow ledge climbing steeply along an exposed rock garden. Concentration is key. At **5.0** miles the route makes an abrupt turn to the east (right) and levels off for a bit. Just ahead on the right is a nice replenishment spot, but since the Katwalk is not far ahead, hit it on the way back. At **5.7** miles reach the Katwalk, a narrow ledge blasted through concrete that's almost guaranteed to annoy your inner acrophobe. Return the way you came.

Alternate Routes

Because this route is on the Pacific Crest Trail, which stretches from Canada to Mexico, the alternate possibilities are endless. A sign at the trailhead reads "Stevens Pass 67," so if you're in the mood for a 134-mile out-and-back run, head for the pass. More likely turnaround points beyond the Kendall Katwalk include Ridge and Gravel Lakes (13 miles out-and-back) or Alaska Mountain (15.5 miles out-and-back).

Nearest Support

Pit toilets are the only trailhead support. Camping is available at the Denny Creek Campground, about 3 miles south of the trailhead off Forest Road 58. Alpine Lakes Wilderness information, 509/548-6977 or www.fs.fed.us/r6/mbs/wilderness/alakes.htm. Food, drink, and accommodations are available about 0.5 mile south of the trailhead at Snoqualmie Pass.

40 Point Defiance Park

PAIN 🏃

GAIN ▲ ▲

Distance	4.7-mile lollipop loop
Elevation gain	500 feet
Time	35 minutes to 1 hour
The route	Wide, easy dirt trail and single track with some pavement. Views. Some signs.
Runnability	100 percent
Season	Year-round
Other users	Hikers
Map	Point Defiance Park Trails (available at park information kiosk)

Warm-up

This beautiful urban park offers an extensive trail network on which to work your trail running mojo. Extending from Tacoma's northern tip into Commencement Bay, the park and its trails offer big-time water and island views. The following route is similar to one favored by members of the Fort Steilacoom Running Club, who meet weekly for organized trail runs.

Approach

From Interstate 5, exit 132, head north on Highway 16 for about 4 miles to Highway 163. Follow this road for 3 miles into the park. The information kiosk and parking area are about 0.25 mile ahead on the right. Elevation: 80 feet.

Go

From the information kiosk, run along the paved road as it bends to the left, then passes in front of the Pagoda. Just ahead, bear right following the sign for 5-Mile Drive. In about 100 yards, follow a trail to the right and run along the far side of a playground. After passing through a stand of trees, run left toward the road while the trail heads right and down. Turn right at the road and run pavement for about 100 yards to the sign for the Rhododendron Garden.

Cross the road and take a quick right on a wide gravel path that climbs gradually. At **0.8** mile, run right at a fork. The trail narrows and becomes more technical as it passes though surprisingly dense forest. A few hundred yards ahead, run right at a four-way intersection, following a signpost with a circle atop a square atop a triangle.

Cross two paved roads in quick succession and at **1.2** miles, turn right at a signpost with only a white square on it. This white square is your beacon for the rest of the run. Cruise downhill for about 0.25 mile before crossing paved 5-Mile Drive. Run left, following the Vashon Photo sign and find the trail reentering the forest just ahead.

Wend your way, winding through a truly fun 0.5-mile stretch of forest. At **2.1** miles, emerge onto paved road and run right for about 15 yards to the next white square escort. Return to the forest for about 200 yards, only to revisit 5-Mile Drive to the Gig Harbor viewpoint. Run left at a picnic shelter on the left side of the road and follow an obvious trail, white square endorsed. (*Note:* This picnic area offers rest rooms and water; no need to carry hydration fluids or liquid-type water stuff.)

Point Defiance Park

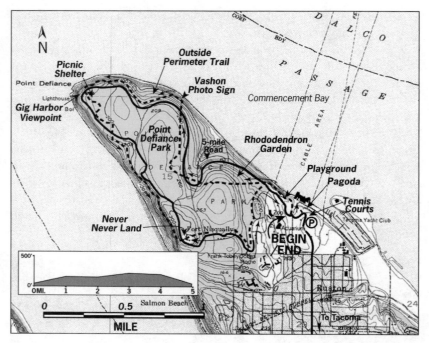

About 150 yards ahead, follow the white square trail to the right at a four-way intersection. For the next 0.75 mile, continue a combination of trail running and brief forays onto pavement. Climb gradually and check out great views of the Tacoma Narrows Bridge and nearby bluffs.

At **3.3** miles, run left as the trail crosses the road between Never Never Land and Fort Nisqually (kind of an odd tandem). The trail drops quickly, crosses a paved road for the umpteenth time, then bears to the right. At **3.8** miles, just before reaching paved road by the zoo parking lot, take a hard left. A few hundred yards ahead, run left again and cruise as the trail widens and continues descending. Reach the Rhododendron Garden sign you passed earlier in the route at **4.2** miles. Return the way you came by turning right.

Nearest Support

Rest rooms, water, and phones are available at the trailhead and at several points on the route. Point Defiance Park information, 253/305-1000 or www.tacomaparks.com. Tacoma offers plenty in the way of food, drink, and accommodations.

41 Margaret McKenny Loop

PAIN 🏃🏃

GAIN ▲▲▲

Distance	7-mile loop
Elevation gain	900 feet
Time	1 to 1.75 hours
The route	Everything from winding, technical single track to wide logging road. Some signs.
Runnability	100 percent
Season	Year-round
Other users	Hikers, bikers, equestrians
Map	DNR Capitol State Forest

Warm-up

This loop at the southeast corner of Capitol State Forest offers a slice of trail-running life in this 90,000-plus acre playground. You experience its mud, its potential for getting runners lost—very high—and get to practice the three E's: equestrian encounter etiquette. Mud levels are at their lowest in July and August.

Approach

Take Interstate 5 to exit 95, about 10 miles south of Olympia. Head west for about 3.6 miles through Littlerock to Waddell Creek Road. Turn right and, 2.4 miles later, left into Margaret McKenny Campground. Follow signs to a large parking area to your left. Elevation: 270 feet.

Go

From the parking lot, head toward the campsites and find the signed Access Trail 6 & 9. Run the well-maintained trail behind the sites, bearing to the left and down when the opportunity presents itself. At **0.4** mile, cross Waddell Creek via a footbridge and begin a short climb to the right. Run right at a T-intersection a few hundred yards ahead.

At **0.7** mile, just before a dirt road, take a hard right onto a single track that at first seems to take you back the way you just came. (Take a look around at

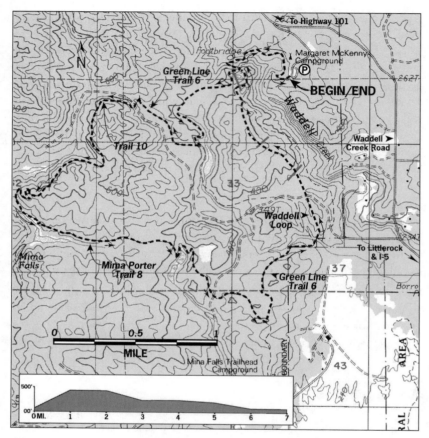

this crossroads area. You'll be coming back here near the end of the route.) Cross a dirt road a few hundred yards ahead.

At **1.1** miles run right onto the wide Green Line Trail 6 at a signed intersection. If it's the rainy season, let the mud wrestling begin. About 0.5 mile farther, at an intersection of trails and road, take a left and cross the road following the sign for Trail 10. The trail is an at-times overgrown-looking single track to the right that heads up. More mud, and if you're lucky, not too much manure, follow. (The first time I ran this route, I came across so many riders on horseback, I thought I'd stumbled into the pages of *Lonesome Dove*.)

At **3.0** miles, merge left onto the Mima Porter Trail 8. Continue winding your way, tiptoeing at times, retrieving your shoes from the mud if necessary. At **4.6** miles, a few hundred yards after crossing a dirt road, run left at a major signed intersection, once again following the sign for Green Line Trail 6.

Traverse a clearcut area, cross a dirt road, and after reentering the forest, ignore a trail to the right that leads to the Evergreen Sportsman's Club.

At **5.2** miles, run right at a T-intersection, following the sign for the Waddell Loop Trail. Just ahead, approach said loop and go left. Follow signs for Waddell Loop, cross several dirt roads, and at **6.3** miles take a left at an intersection, following the sign for McKenny Camp. A few hundred yards ahead, find yourself at the crossroads intersection you encountered at the 0.7-mile mark. This time cross the dirt road and pick up the Green Line Trail 6 across the way. Follow for a few hundred yards and take a right at another intersection you navigated earlier in the route. Return to the parking lot the way you came.

Nearest Support

Margaret McKenny Campground offers water, portable toilets, telephones, and camping. Park information, 800/527-3305. The small town of Littlerock, about 5 miles west of the park, offers basic food and drinks. For more options, including accommodations, Olympia is about 16 miles north of the trailhead off I-5.

42

TACOMA / OLYMPIA
Capitol Peak

PAIN 🏃🏃🏃
GAIN ▲▲▲▲

Distance	8.2 miles out and back
Elevation gain	1,700 feet
Time	1 to 1.75 hours
The route	Forested single track, wide trail, and logging road along a ridge. Views. Some signs.
Runnability	100 percent
Season	Year-round
Other users	Hikers, bikers, equestrians
Map	DNR Capitol State Forest

Warm-up

On clear days, this route pays off in big ways—heart-stopping views of every Washington volcano, the Olympics, *and* the Pacific Ocean: not too shabby. However, with the heavy-duty trucks that rumble up and down Capitol State Forest's dirt roads, getting to the trailhead can seem a bit hairy at times. Use caution, especially when approaching blind bends in the road. The views from up top are worth it.

Approach

Take Interstate 5 to exit 88, about 17 miles south of Olympia. Head west on Highway 12 for about 18 miles to easy-to-miss C-Line Road on your right. Drive the winding dirt and gravel road for about 8.5 miles to Camp Wedekind, a picnic area and horse camp. Just before reaching a shelter, find a gated dirt road to the left and a trailhead sign pointing the way to Capitol Peak. Park here. Elevation: 1,880 feet.

Go

From the Capitol Peak sign, find the trail leading into the forest and begin climbing immediately. This is Trail 30, not that this knowledge will get you very far. At **0.5** mile, take a right onto Green Line Trail 6 and bounce along a soft dirt single track watching out for hoof-sized holes that mark the trail

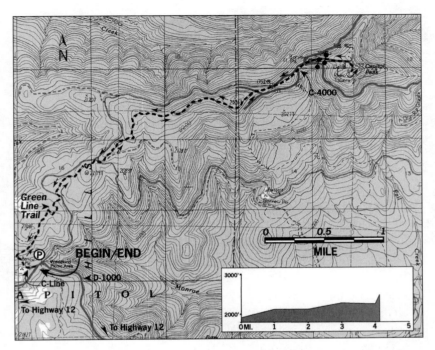

from time to time. Cross a dirt road at about 1.1 miles, rejoining the trail on the other side about 20 yards to the left.

Come to a multi-way dirt road intersection in a little more than 0.5 mile. Take a right and run about 100 yards, crossing a road in the process. Find a horse-trail sign a few yards farther on the left and head up into the woods. Capitol State Forest has a reputation for being a great place to run and ride, as well as get lost, so take comfort in the Green Line Trail 6 signs that pop up along the route. Continue climbing gradually along a ridge that offers wonderful views from time to time.

At 3.2 miles, just after a short, steep stretch, the trail takes a sharp turn to the right and descends for a bit. Just before intersecting with another dirt road, the trail veers left and continues on mostly level ground for a few hundred yards. Come to another multi-way dirt road intersection, and this time cross the road and pick up the trail on the other side. Descend for about 0.3 mile. Soon the trail pops out onto a dirt road, C-4000. Run along the road until you come to three prongs of a dirt road fork. The two roads to the right are gated. Run up the middle road and reach the summit with its attendant

views galore in a few hundred yards at **4.1** miles. Eat, drink, gawk. Return the
way you came, having fun the whole downhill way back.

Nearest Support

Wedekind Camp offers pit toilets. Capitol State Forest offers several campgrounds. Park information, 800/527-3305. The town of Oakville, about 12
miles south of Wedekind, offers basic food and drinks. For more options,
including accommodations, Olympia is off I-5 about 40 miles north.

43 Millersylvania State Park

PAIN 🏃

GAIN ▲ ▲

Distance	3.1-mile loop
Elevation gain	130 feet
Time	25 to 45 minutes
The route	Wide, flat forest trail, dirt road, and paved campground road. Few signs.
Runnability	100 percent
Season	Year-round
Other users	Hikers, bikers
Map	Millersylvania State Park (available at park office)

Warm-up

This park's gentle forest route is perfect for beginning trail runners or experienced ones looking for the yin to nearby Capitol State Forest's yang. In summer, cool off after your run with a refreshing dip in Deep Lake.

Approach

Take Interstate 5 to exit 95, about 10 miles south of Olympia. Head east for 2.6 miles on Maytown Road (Highway 121), following signs for the park. Take a left at a T-intersection with Tilley Road. The park is 0.8 mile ahead on the left. Park in the day use area just ahead to the left. Elevation: 200 feet.

Go

Find the trail signpost across from the park office near the park entrance and set off on the wide and cushy forest trail. At **0.4** mile, just after crossing a dirt road, enter the Fitness Trail. It's one of those '70s-era par-course thingees that entreats you to stop mid-run to tiptoe across a balance beam, lunge like a fencer, jump on one leg, and other such behaviors. Feel free to ignore such instructions while you run the trail.

About 0.25 mile farther, take a right at a T-intersection. A few hundred yards ahead, do the same thing. At **1.2** miles, take yet another right onto a dirt road at yet another T-intersection. In fewer than two shakes, an erroneous sign at an intersection with a trail to the left says the lake is 3 miles to the left, the

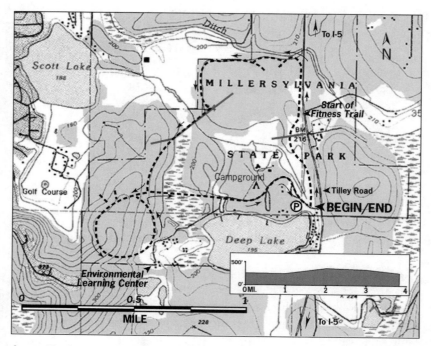

forest 4 miles straight ahead. Actually, it's 0.3 and .04 respectively. Keep running the dirt road, and at **1.6** miles go straight on forest trail when the road veers right.

Open 'er up on this wide, soft stretch. About 0.25 mile ahead, take a right following the sign for ELC (Environmental Learning Center). Remember this spot for you'll be returning here. Just ahead, take a left, again guided by the ELC sign, and run a 0.6-mile forest loop that touches the edge of the ELC's grounds. When the trail opens up to reveal the grounds, keep to the left, where you will soon find the trail when it reenters the forest.

After taking a left at a T-intersection with a dirt road, complete the loop and take a right. Just ahead, run straight at the intersection you came to just before the ELC loop, following the (correct) sign that says "Lake, 0.4 mile." Parts of the following stretch can be not only muddy but under several inches of water, so make sure your shoes are tied tight. At **2.8** miles, ignore a trail leading to the left. Just ahead, the trail comes to an end at the paved campground road. Run the road back to where you parked, bearing to the left at one point near the campground's RV section.

Nearest Support

Millersylvania State Park offers rest rooms, water, telephones, and camping. Information, 360/753-1519 or www.parks.wa.gov/miller.htm. Olympia, which offers much in the way of food, drink, and accommodations, is off I-5 about 14 miles north of the trailhead.

44 Ipsut Creek–Spray Park Loop

PAIN 🏃🏃🏃🏃🏃

GAIN ▲▲▲▲▲

Distance	16.6-mile lollipop loop
Elevation gain	4,550 feet
Time	3 to 5 hours
The route	Soft forest trail and technical single track to rough moraine. Views. Well-signed.
Alternate route	8.5-mile out and back from Mowich Lake to Spray Park.
Runnability	80 percent
Season	July to October
Other users	Hikers
Map	Green Trails Mount Rainier West 269
Permit	Northwest Forest Pass
Fees	Mount Rainier National Park entrance fee—$10 per car, $5 per individual

Warm-up

Side A of this route includes long steep climbs through rich, dense forest with massive trees; Side B offers screaming descents and wildflower meadows that'll make you croon *The Sound of Music* theme whether you want to or not. The B-side also features Mount Rainier, so big and so close as to seem almost unreal.

Approach

Enter Mount Rainier National Park at the Carbon River entrance. From Highway 165, about 11 miles south of Buckley, turn left onto Carbon River Road at a fork and drive about 8 miles to the Carbon River Ranger Station. From the ranger station, drive about 5 miles on a dirt road to the Ipsut Creek Campground. Find the trailhead parking lot at the far end of the campground. *Note:* Seasonal floods sometimes wash out Carbon River Road. Call the ranger station or check the Web site for the latest conditions. Elevation: 2,300 feet.

Go

From the trailhead kiosk, head out on the wide, soft trail through deep forest. About 0.25 mile in, run left at the Ipsut Falls sign. At a fork just ahead, run

Crossing a snow patch near Spray Park

right following the sign for Mowich Lake. You're on the Wonderland Trail now, my friend, and will be for about the next 5 miles.

With the trail narrowing and becoming more overrun with rocks and roots, start your first climb of the day. Serenaded by rushing Ipsut Creek to your right, accumulate elevation—sometimes steeply, sometimes gradually— past giant firs and hemlocks. At **2.8** miles, emerge from the forest in the center of a great meadow-like amphitheater, surrounded by forested slopes and craggy peaks.

Cross a creek and begin a serious climb through meadow, forest, and scree slopes. How *serious?* About 1,000 feet worth over the next mile. Pass directly below Tolmie Peak's impressive rock face and at **3.8** miles reach Ipsut Pass. Run left. A fun downhill and level stretch on soft, wide trail follows, culminating in 1.5 miles at Mowich Lake. Take in the route's first Mount Rainier sighting while enjoying a sips-'n'-munches break on the lakeshore.

At the south end of Lake Mowich, run right at the T-intersection and follow the sign for Spray Park. Pass through Mowich Lake Camp, find the Spray Park Trail sign, and after reentering the forest begin dropping quickly. Before you start feeling too good about this deserved downhill, however, be aware that you still have more than 1,500 feet of climbing ahead of you. At **6.2** miles, run left at a fork following the sign for Spray Park. Bid the Wonderland Trail adieu.

Cross a couple of creeks via log bridges, pass through a rock garden, and start climbing again. In about 0.75 mile, continue straight at a signed turnoff to the right for Spray Falls. Gain mucho elevation over the next 0.5 mile on a rocky and wet stretch of trail that eventually coughs you out into the wildflower heaven that is Spray Park. Glorious, magnificent, splendiferous, and a bunch of other superlatives that I've never used in actual conversation don't do justice to this magical mix of mountain and meadow. Along with the obvious—Rainier to the south—views extend north all the way to the North Cascades.

Continue climbing, albeit more gradually, crossing the occasional snow patch and some rough moraine. Look for cairns and a boot trail if the way is snow-covered. At **9.7** miles, the trail takes a turn toward the north and begins dropping quickly. Feel free to be smug about it. All today's climbing is behind you. Much of the trail is narrow, winding, rocky, and root-filled, so resist the urge to break the sound barrier. Views—mountains, flowers, forest—are distracting anyway, as are the numerous creek crossings.

Continue busting those quads on this relentless downhill, ignoring the Cataract Camp sign at **12.3** miles. Now running through forest, do the downhill switchback thing for about 0.5 mile before the long straight descent toward the Carbon River. At **13.8** miles, rejoin the Wonderland Trail, following the sign for Ipsut Campground. Almost immediately, cross a creek on a log bridge and, just ahead, meet up with the Carbon River. Run along the river's floodplain on mostly level, old roadbed and just marvel at what you've seen today—mountain, meadow, forest, flowers, and sheer power, as in the river beside you.

Return to the forest and at **16.3** miles bid the Wonderland good-bye, bear to the right, and rerun the 0.3 mile of trail you started with back to Ipsut Campground.

Alternate Route

For an 8.5-mile out-and-back run to Spray Park, start at Mowich Lake. To get to Mowich Lake, follow the directions above, but at the fork 11 miles south of Buckley, bear right and follow the sign for the Mowich Lake entrance.

Nearest Support

Pit toilets and water are available at Ipsut Creek Campground near the trailhead. Pit toilets, but not water, are also available at Mowich Lake Camp. Mount Rainier National Park information, 360/569-2211 or www.nps.gov/mora. Food, drink, and accommodations are available in Buckley, about 25 miles north of the trailhead off Highway 165.

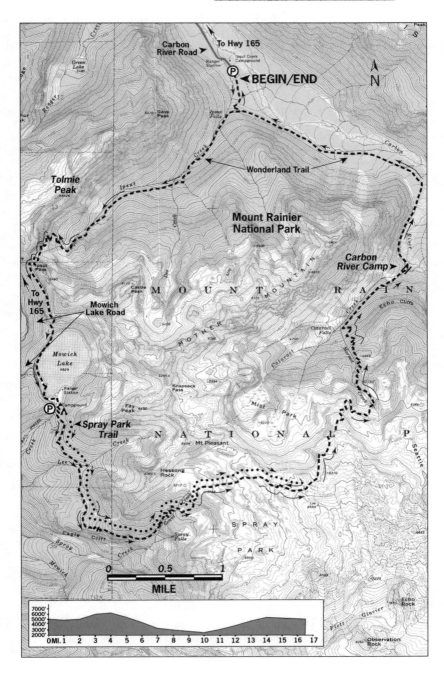

45 Camp Sheppard–Forest Shelter Loop

PAIN 🏃🏃🏃🏃
GAIN ▲▲▲▲

Distance	14.5-mile loop
Elevation gain	2,950 feet
Time	2 to 3.5 hours
The route	Technical and non-technical single track through forest and along scenic ridge. Views. Signs.
Runnability	90 percent
Season	July to October
Other users	Hikers, bikers, equestrians
Map	Green Trails Greenwater 238
Permit	Northwest Forest Pass

Warm-up

This route, part of the White River 50 Mile Trail Run course, throws you some steep mega-climbs as well as one long, fast downhill. You lose about 2,500 feet over 5 continuous downhill miles, so hold onto your chapeaus and toupees. The ridge-top views of the White River, as it snakes its way through evergreen foothills on the lam from Mount Rainier, are extraordinary.

Approach

From Enumclaw, drive south on Highway 410 for about 28 miles. Just past milepost 52, find the Camp Sheppard Boy Scout Camp trailhead on the left. Park here. Elevation: 2,450 feet.

Go

To the left of the kiosk, start by running on a wide gravel trail. Pass through a clearing, reenter the forest, and continue straight at a fork near a meeting place. Just ahead, where the new trail bears to the right, run straight up an old dirt road. At **0.3** mile, reach a trail intersection and run left following the sign for The Dalles Creek Trail.

Run a mostly level stretch in and out of forest and continue straight at a four-way intersection. At **1.3** miles, run right at a T-intersection following the

Ridgetop views from Camp Sheppard-Forest Shelter Loop

sign for the Palisade Trail (1198). Say good-bye to easy street and begin a bru-tal, technical climb that gains about 800 feet in little more a mile. Switchback beneath some huge rock walls, pass a couple of waterfalls, climb one of the steepest flights of wood steps you'll ever come across, and at **2.7** miles, be rewarded with the first of the day's ridge-top views. Check out Sun Top, the White River, and Mount Rainier, views of which become even more dra-matic as the route progresses.

Return to the forest and resume climbing, though not at the insanity that as you did previously. Over the next 5 miles, pop out onto the ridge, then back into the forest a number of times, with each popout a few hundred feet higher—and with a better view—than the previous one. One or two ridge popouts extend for a few hundred yards and offer 1,500 feet of air in exchange for a misstep to the right. Unless you can fly, don't misstep.

At **7.9** miles, with the route's last popout behind you, come to a shelter and a signed intersection with Trail 1197. Take a hard right and hang on to your bonnet. Drop quickly down steep, ledge-like single track that soon enough turns into long, wide sweeping downhill stretches. It'll convince you that you haven't lost the speed you had when you were eighteen after all. At **9.9** miles, run straight at the Ranger Creek Trail sign and continue amazing yourself with your newfound speed—or feeling sorry for the pounding you're giving your poor quads.

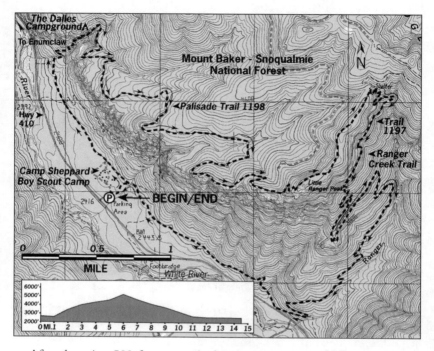

After dropping 500 feet per mile for about 5 miles, at **12.7** miles make a hard right at a signed intersection and start heading back north to Camp Sheppard. The trail drops quickly then levels off as it approaches and then parallels Highway 410. Run straight at a couple of signed intersections until returning to the intersection you hit at the 0.3-mile mark. Turn left here and return to the parking lot the way you came.

Nearest Support

Pit toilets are the only trailhead support. Camping is available at The Dalles Campground, about 2 miles north of Camp Sheppard on Highway 410. Mount Baker–Snoqualmie National Forest information, 360/825-6585 or www.fs.fed.us/r6/mbs/index.html. Greenwater, about 10 miles north of Camp Sheppard, offers food, drink, and accommodations.

46

Wonderland to Panhandle Gap

PAIN 🏃🏃🏃🏃

GAIN ▲▲▲▲▲

Distance	11.4 miles out and back
Elevation gain	3,000 feet
Time	1.5 to 2.75 hours
The route	Soft forest trail and single track to rough moraine. Creek and snow crossings. Views. Signs.
Alternate route	17-mile point to point to Box Canyon
Runnability	95 percent
Season	July to October
Other users	Hikers
Map	Green Trails Mount Rainier East 270
Permit	Northwest Forest Pass
Fees	Mount Rainier National Park entrance fee—$10 per car, $5 per individual

Warm-up

This great Mount Rainier route takes you from dense forest to flower-filled meadows to glacier toe. Run along rushing, and at times, roaring Fryingpan Creek, get whistled at by cheeky marmots hiding behind a rainbow of wildflowers, gaze upon glaciated Mounts Adams and Hood from 6,800-foot Panhandle Gap. All in all, this is a spectacular way to spend the day.

Approach

From Enumclaw, head south on Highway 410 for about 37 miles to the White River entrance of Mount Rainier National Park. The trailhead is about 4 miles ahead on the left, just across the Fryingpan Creek bridge. Elevation: 3,800 feet.

Go

From the trailhead, run through cool forest on the wide, mostly level trail. A few hundred yards in, merge with the Wonderland Trail, that 95-mile ring of fun that circles the mountain. At about 1.7 miles, begin climbing as the trail switchbacks alongside sizzling Fryingpan Creek. About 0.75 mile ahead, and

Rainier views from Panhandle Gap

400 feet higher, Rainier's frosty white head shows up with Little Tahoma looking not so little.

At **3.2** miles, cross Fryingpan Creek via a log bridge and pass through a lush land of avalanche lilies. Soon, however, reenter the forest and begin a steep series of switchbacks on which you climb 700 feet in less than a mile. At **4.2** miles, reach Summerland Camp where the mountain and meadow views are simply glorious, if one can use such a phrase and not be accused of being a sissy. The sheer size of the place is enough to take one's breath away. Consider this a great place to sip and slurp before carrying on to rockier stuff.

Back on the trail, descend for a bit, cross a stream, and begin the various creek, snow, and boulder crossings that come with running across a moraine. Follow cairns if and when the trail is hard to follow and boot tracks when snow is in the way. If the route is icy, don't proceed—you can slide a long way up here. At **5.7** miles, you'll reach Panhandle Gap. Gaze south on clear days and give a shout to Mounts Adams and Hood. Return the way you came.

Alternate Route

For a 17-mile point-to-point run, park one car near Fryingpan Creek as described above and the other at the Box Canyon parking lot. Run the route to Panhandle Gap but instead of turning around there, continue running south on the Wonderland Trail. In about 8 miles run right at the intersection with the Olallie Trail and remain on the Wonderland. Reach the Box Canyon parking lot in about 3 more miles.

To get to the Box Canyon parking lot, enter Mount Rainier National Park at the Stevens Canyon entrance. The parking lot is about 10 miles ahead on the right.

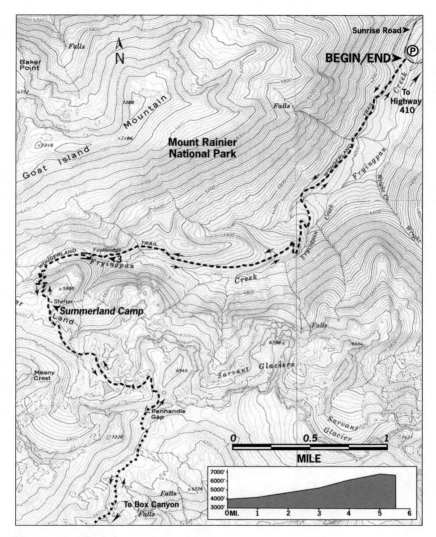

Nearest Support

This route's trailhead offers no water or rest rooms, though Summerland Camp offers a pit toilet. Mount Rainier National Park information, 360/569-2211 or out www.nps.gov/mora. Greenwater, about 25 miles north of the trailhead, offers food, drink, and accommodations.

OLYMPIC PENINSULA
47 Elk Mountain

PAIN 🏃🏃🏃🏃🏃
GAIN ▲▲▲▲▲

Distance	15.2 miles out and back
Elevation gain	3,450 feet
Time	2.25 to 4 hours
The route	Single track through alpine environment, much of it above tree line. Views. Signs.
Alternate route	7.6 miles point to point
Runnability	90 percent
Season	July to September
Other users	Hikers
Permit	Northwest Forest Pass
Map	Green Trails Mount Angeles 135

Warm-up

This spectacular ridge run gets you above tree line and the clouds so quickly you'll swear you're flying. All around you is an amazing array of places to fly to: ridges leading in all directions, majestic Mount Olympus and the other

Obstruction Point Trail

Olympians, even the Strait of Juan de Fuca. A bunch of dips and doodles on the route ensure that there's plenty of hill climbing each way.

Approach

Drive west on U.S. 101 to just before milepost 253, about 3 miles west of Port Angeles. Turn left on Deer Park Road and follow it for almost 17 miles to the sign for the Obstruction Point Trail. (Eleven miles of the road, which gains almost 5,000 feet in elevation, is dirt, and much of it is winding and rough.) Turn right and park in the small lot by a ranger station about 100 yards ahead. Elevation: 5,200 feet.

Go

From the trailhead kiosk, start by dropping about 350 feet over the first 0.75 mile on a wide forested trail. This is a nice way to warm up but, as you'll find out later, a cruel way to finish. Once the trail bottoms out, you'll immediately start gaining new elevation. Following along the ridge of Green Mountain, the first couple of miles of trail climb steadily but also throw in a fair amount of downhill.

At **2.7** miles, the trees thin out and the views begin in earnest. Craggy Maiden Peak, dressed in wildflower meadows, is straight ahead. Olympian peaks, glaciers, and ridges dominate the south, lowlands and civilization the north. Climb gradually while passing through meadow, rocky scree slopes, and a thin stand of trees on your way to rounding a bend at **3.3** miles. Here the views get really dramatic—Hamlet dramatic—and they stay that way for the rest of the route. Except for a few hearty trees, the forest is now below you so there's nothing to block the views—or the sun, so remember the sunblock. Have fun tracing the folds and ridges of outrageous mountains. And you thought Ruffles had a lot of ridges.

About 0.5 mile ahead, begin a steep, slippery, rocky descent to the signed Roaring Winds Camp. The few trees and large rocks offer some shelter from the wind (if needed) and a place to sit and sip if you're in need. Look for ptarmigan that love to blend into the area's rocks and meadows. Just ahead, start climbing a steep, slippery, rock-studded slope to the upper reaches of Elk Mountain. At **5.5** miles, reach the trail's high point (6,600 feet) and the signed intersection with the trail to Badger Valley. Run right, following the arrow for Obstruction Point.

Traverse on a mostly level plane for about a mile before dropping about 400 feet across a sketchy scree slope and, at **7.4** miles, another signed intersection

OLYMPIC PENINSULA

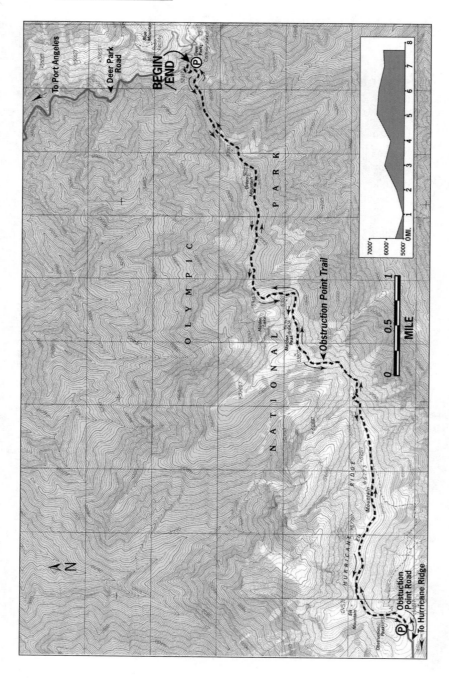

To Port Angeles

Deer Park Road

BEGIN/END

Deer Park Campground

Blue Mountain

OLYMPIC

NATIONAL

PARK

Green Mountain

Obstruction Point Trail

Maiden Peak

Maiden Peak

HURRICANE RIDGE

Elk Mountain

Obstruction Point

Obstruction Point Road

To Hurricane Ridge

N

7000'
5000'
5000'
OMI. 1 2 3 4 5 6 7 8

0   0.5   1
MILE

158

with a trail to Badger Valley. Just ahead, round a bend on a wide ledge. In 0.2 mile, arrive at the Obstruction Point parking lot, which, given the seeming remoteness of where you've been running, will seem quite odd.

Eat, drink, and enjoy. Prepare for the way back. Because you ran downhill for 1,300-plus feet to get here (as well as uphill for almost 2,200) this won't be your usual downhill coast on the way back, but the scenery is stunning enough that you won't mind.

Alternate Route

For a 7.6 mile point-to-point run, park one car at Deer Park and the other at Obstruction Point. For more downhill running, start at Obstruction Point. To get to Obstruction Point, in Port Angeles pick up the 17-mile highway to Hurricane Ridge. Just before the Hurricane Ridge Visitor Center, turn left on dirt Obstruction Point Road and follow it for almost 8 miles to Obstruction Point parking lot.

Nearest Support

The Deer Park area and Obstruction Point offer pit toilets but not water. Camping is permitted at the Deer Park Campground near the trailhead. Olympic National Park information, 360/452-0329 or www.nps.gov/olym. For food, drink, and places to stay, Port Angeles is 20 miles north off U.S. 101.

48 Spruce Railroad Trail

PAIN 🏃🏃

GAIN ▲ ▲ ▲

Distance	8.2 miles out and back
Elevation gain	330 feet
Time	1 to 1.75 hours
The route	Lakeside single track and wide trail on abandoned railroad grade. Views. Signs.
Runnability	100 percent
Season	Year-round
Other users	Hikers, bikers
Permit	Northwest Forest Pass
Map	Green Trails Lake Crescent 101

Warm-up

This easy trail follows part of the shoreline of 12-mile-long Lake Crescent, the third largest natural body of water in the state. The doppelganger of Aurora Ridge, which looms over the lake from the south, and its reflection in the lake, is a real stunner and provides much inspiration. Though most of this route is wide and tame, some narrow stretches are made tricky by rockfall.

Approach

Drive west on U.S. 101 to just past milepost 232 and East Beach Road. Turn right and in 3.2 miles take a left following the sign for the Spruce Railroad Trail. The trail is about 0.9 mile ahead. Elevation: 600 feet.

Go

Find the wide forested trail just behind the information kiosk and begin a gradual climb. At about **0.5** mile, just after the trail levels off, start descending to the lakeshore, while views open up to the left. Bounce along the wood bridge at **1.2** miles and allow the high Wow! factor of Aurora Ridge reflecting in the emerald lake to dazzle you. You'll likely have no choice.

Over the next 3 miles to the turnaround, the trail is pretty straightforward and easy to follow. Between 2.0 and 3.0 miles, run through some stretches of rockfall. At **4.1** miles, just after veering left at a fork by a privy, reach a dirt road

Crescent Lake and Aurora Ridge

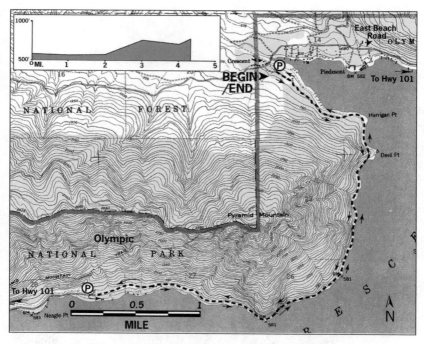

and the west trailhead for the Spruce Railroad Trail. Turn around and return the way you came.

Nearest Support

A privy is the only trailhead support. Olympic National Park information, 360/452-4501 or www.nps.gov/olym/home.htm. Olympic National Park has numerous campgrounds and campsites. For food, drinks, and further accommodations, Port Angeles is about 15 miles east off U.S. 101.

49 OLYMPIC PENINSULA
Ozette Trails

PAIN 🏃🏃

GAIN ▲▲▲▲▲

Distance	9.3-mile loop
Elevation gain	550 feet
Time	1.25 to 2.25 hours
The route	Forested wood plank trail and sandy beach. Two short sections of technical single track. Views. Signs.
Runnability	100 percent
Season	Year-round
Other users	Hikers
Permit	Northwest Forest Pass
Map	Green Trails Ozette 130S

Warm-up

One of the most unusual routes in this collection in that it entails fewer than 200 yards of dirt trail. The rest is forgiving, if potentially slippery, wood planks and sandy beach along the Pacific Ocean and all the cool things that implies— crashing waves, sea stacks, tidal pools, petroglyphs, eagles—and of course the sensation that one is running on sand. Find the firmest part of the beach and go for it.

Special Considerations: It's safest not to run this trail near high tide when the rising water makes two stretches of the beach potentially dangerous. At these points, find the short, steep headland trails—indicated by black-and-orange circular signs—that lead up into bluffs and past the sketchy sections. Check the tide tables at the trailhead interpretive kiosk or talk to the ranger before heading out.

Approach

Drive west on U.S. 101 to Sappho, about 43 miles west of Port Angeles. Take a right on Highway 113 and continue north for 9 miles to Highway 112. Turn left and drive about 9 miles, just past Sekiu to Ozette Lake Road. Drive 21 miles to the ranger station at road's end. Elevation: 40 feet.

Ozette boardwalk to the beach

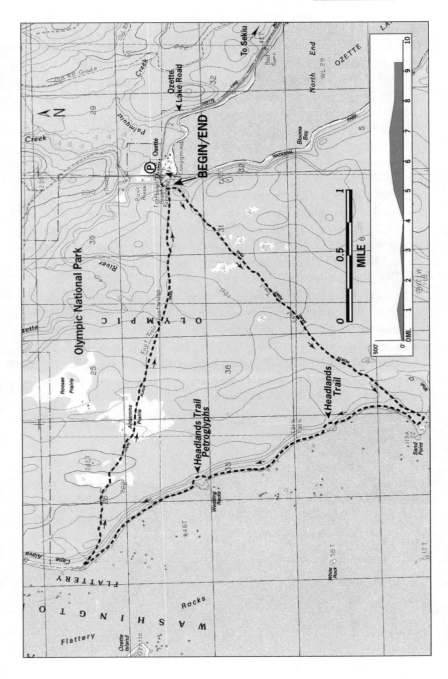

Go

From the ranger station and information hut, cross the Ozette River via a bridge. Just ahead, run left following the sign for Sand Point. After a short stretch of dirt and gravel trail, hop aboard the wood plank boardwalk trail. This fun, bouncy surface is your yellow brick road all the way to the ocean. It's a great surface, but it can be slippery when wet.

Snake your way through thick forest and dense undergrowth—greenery at all levels—until reaching the beach at **3.0** miles. Stop and stare at waves crashing upon sea stacks, tide pools bubbling with mini-worlds of their own, eagles soaring overhead, seals playing in the surf. Then take a right. Find the sand/rock/pebble surface that offers your feet the best grip and let 'er rip northward as best you can. It's likely to be slow going for some stretches but so what. There's plenty to look at, including rapidly changing weather. When I ran this route in mid-July 2000, I experienced chilly temperatures, driving rain, and howling winds interspersed with short periods of hot sun and blue sky, all in about a half hour's time.

At about **4.8** miles, if the tide makes running around some blocky sea stacks seem too dangerous, find the orange-and-black disk sign pointing to a headlands trail. A short, steep, rocky trail—with a rope for negotiating the slipperiest section—offers a way around. Before heading up, however, check out the petroglyphs of whales and passing ships etched onto the rocks. A little more than a mile farther, reach Cape Alava and spot another orange-and-black disk. Find the trail and, after waving good-bye to the Pacific Ocean, head back to the headlands. Return to the Ozette Ranger Station on another 3-plus miles of bouncy boardwalk.

Nearest Support

Rest rooms, water, and telephones are available at the Ozette traihead. Ozette Ranger Station information, 360/963-2725 or www.nps.gov/olym/home.htm. Sekiu, which offers more in the food, gas, and lodging departments, is about 30 miles north on Highway 112.

50 MOUNT ST. HELENS
Loowit Trail
PAIN 🏃🏃🏃🏃🏃
GAIN ▲▲▲▲▲

Distance	32.7-mile lollipop loop
Elevation gain	6,600 feet
Time	8 to 14 hours
The route	Technical single track and hard-to-follow trail through boulder fields, desert, forest, and more. Views. Well-signed.
Runnability	70 percent
Season	July to October
Other users	Hikers, mountain bikers
Permit	Northwest Forest Pass
Maps	Green Trails Mount St. Helens NW 364S; Geo-Graphics Mount St. Helens Recreation Map

Warm-up

Want an amazing trail-running experience while taking a crash course on volcanology at the same time? Run the Loowit Loop, which circumscribes Mount St. Helens and offers glimpses into this volcano's crater and its many moods—all of them. You'll scramble atop boulder-strewn lava flows, pick your way across pumice- and ash-covered deserts, cross snowfield-fed creeks, maneuver through sketchy canyons, and more. This route easily provides the most arduous adventure in this book.

Special Considerations: The route crosses many creeks, but only a few are safe for drinking. At about mile 13, the Toutle River, though a bit silty, is safe as long as you filter or pill it. For better water, turn left just before the Toutle River at the intersection with the Toutle Trail (Trail 238) and run about 0.25 mile to a much clearer creek. At mile 21.6, a spring that emerges from the ground just to right of the trail offers the best water on the route. A creek about 4.5 miles beyond that, just after Pumice Butte, is another fine water source.

Call the ranger for the latest trail conditions and for the latest on water issues. This is a long and potentially hot day, and you will spend much time crossing a desert, so be sure to get an early start.

Mount St. Helens Crater on Loowit Trail

Approach

Take Interstate 5 south to exit 21 in Woodland. Head east on Highway 503 for about 23 miles to the intersection with 503 Spur by Jack's Restaurant. Continue straight on 503 Spur for about 7 miles to the intersection with Forest Road 83. Turn left and continue for 5.5 miles to the signed June Lake trailhead on the left. Elevation: 2,720 feet.

Go

Proceed up the soft, wide, gradually ascending June Lake Trail for about 1.4 miles to pristine June Lake. Ooh and aah at the plunging 70-foot waterfall, then follow the trail as it climbs straight into the old growth forest. Just ahead, bear left at an unsigned T-intersection with a short spur that leads to a closer view of the waterfall. At 1.7 miles, come to a signed T-intersection with the Loowit Trail (Trail 216), your personal magic carpet for the rest of the day. Next time you see this Loowit Trail sign, you're likely to be thinking about how much you're going to eat and drink tonight, all without guilt.

Take a left and soon enough introduce yourself to the first of many lava flows, a recurring theme on the south side of the mountain. The hard-to-follow trail winds its way through large black, blocky boulders requiring not only a slow pace but also the use of hands in certain sections. Look for tall wood posts that mark the sometimes-obscure trail, or cairns—small stacks of

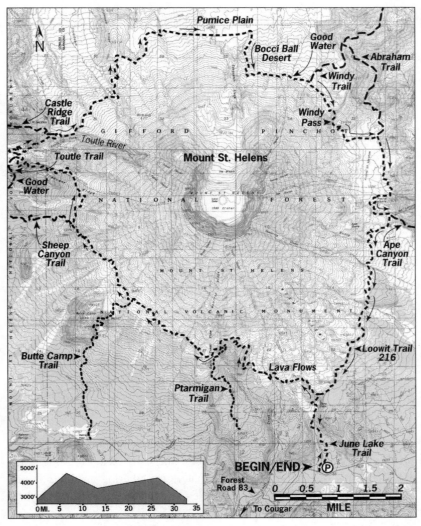

rocks—placed by those who've gone before you. (These two bits of advice will serve you well the entire route.)

After about 0.5 mile, leave the lava flow and run through what seems like a more typical mountain environment—except for the volcanic ash, rock, and other signs of destruction. Climb steadily through forests, meadows, and other natural wonders. Reach the first of another of the route's recurring themes: a canyon crossing. Negotiating these gorges, which are 40 to 100 feet deep, and which emanate from the top of the mountain like spokes from the hub of a wheel, generally involve the following: a tricky descent down an unstable ash and mud canyon wall; a rushing creek or dry riverbed crossing, followed by an equally sketchy ascent up the opposite wall of the canyon. On some crossings, it's not readily apparent where the trail resumes up the opposite wall. Keep looking. You'll eventually find it. The Loowit Trail offers countless canyon crossings. Lava-flow crossings come and go too. Expect 100- to 200-yard snow crossings as well, something I encountered a number of times at 4,300 feet and above when I ran this route in late July 2000.

At **4.7** miles, merge temporarily with the Ptarmigan Trail (216A). Bear right. Just ahead, bear left, following the sign for Trail 216 (Loowit Trail). Creek and lava crossings follow, as do stunning views of not only this volcanic wonder you're running around but also Mount Hood to the south and Mount Adams to the east. As the trail levels off a little, take time to appreciate the rainbow of wildflowers that pop up when they have a chance. At **6.9** miles, reach the intersection with the Butte Camp Trail (238A). Follow the sign for Trail 216 and continue a mostly level traverse—save for the ubiquitous stream and gorge crossings—at or just above tree level. Some good running can be had here.

Reach the intersection with the Sheep Canyon Trail (240) at **9.1** miles. Not long after, begin to give back much of that elevation you gained earlier. Descend about 1,500 feet on your way through old growth forest into the Toutle River Valley, checking out the stupendous views of the river and sur-rounding hills on the way down. Try not to think about how you've got to make back all this elevation and then some. At **13.1** miles reach the intersec-tion with the Toutle Trail (238) and bear right. A short stretch of bushwacking quickly follows, and then you're on the banks of the Toutle River. Negotiate yet another canyon and probably the widest and fastest water crossing of the day. The Toutle River, though silty, is potable after filtering or pilling it with iodine tablets. Another option is to run left at the Toutle Trail and follow for about 0.25 mile to a less silty creek.

Back at the Toutle River, find the trail about 100 yards upriver on the far riverbank. Look for boot prints, flags, cairns, or other trail markers. Begin climbing out of the river valley almost immediately. Traverse a steep pumice slope on which running is difficult, if not impossible, because of the sandy surface on which you'll tend to lean heavily to the left just to stay upright—a real challenge for those inclined to vertigo. At **14.4** miles, run right at the intersection with the Castle Ridge Trail (216G). Continue climbing, wowed by the views opening up to the north—the Blast Zone's Pumice Plain backed by Johnston Ridge and Mount Rainier beyond.

The sand and pumice desert landscape that follows is punctuated with gullies galore and multicolored rocks the size of bocci balls that make the trail extremely difficult to follow—as do the stunning views deep into the volcano's crater. This section, named the "Bocci Ball Desert" by a companion and me, has no posts to follow, only cairns that are difficult to distinguish from naturally occurring rock piles. Also distracting are the views of Spirit Lake and its surrounding hills, covered with millions of downed trees that resemble toothpicks.

At **20.0** miles, run right as the trail leaves the "Bocci Ball Desert" and begins climbing directly toward the crater. *Note:* When we ran this route, we noticed a wood post lying on the ground at this turn. Most likely, it was about to be installed and, hopefully, there is now a post marking the trail. Continue climbing for about a mile, ignoring two trails in fairly quick succession that lead to the right.

At **21.6** miles, reach a spring that bubbles up out of the mountain just to the right of the trail. Resist the temptation to guzzle for hours while gazing into Spirit Lake and head on. Just ahead, bear right at the Windy Trail (216E) and make your way toward Windy Pass (4,885 feet), the highest point on the route. The narrow trail up the steep, but fairly short, climb requires your best mountain-goat impression, the sandy, rocky descent your concentration. Check out the Plains of Abraham spread out before you and glacier-draped Mount Adams looming large to the east.

Follow cairns and obvious trail across the flat, scrubby desert to the intersection with the Abraham Trail (216D) at **24.2** miles. Run right and head south, continuing what's been another good stretch of level running on easy-to-follow trail. Just after sneaking a peak down deep Ape Canyon and whistling at a marmot or two, follow the trail as it bears right. At **26.0** miles, reach the intersection with the Ape Canyon Trail (234). Head right. If a trail such as this can be said to have a home stretch, this is where it would start. Unfortunately, with 800 more feet of elevation gain and five deep canyon and creek crossings, not to mention a lava flow or two, these last 5 miles of the Loowit Trail are not very much like a home stretch. (They also seem a lot longer than 5 miles.)

At **31.0** miles reach the T-intersection with the June Lake Trail and plant a big kiss on the sign for the June Lake trailhead, which is 1.7 downhill miles away. Return the way you came. Consider a post-Loowit dip into cool, clear June Lake.

Eat.

Drink.

Nearest Support

The June Lake trailhead offers no services. Mount St. Helens National Volcanic Monument offers no campgrounds, though there are several just outside the park. Information, 360/247-3955 or www.fs.fed/us/gpnf/mshnvm. Cougar, a very small town about 8 miles east, offers food and accommodations.

Resources

General Information

Alpine Lakes Wilderness: 509/548-6977; www.fs.fed.us/r6/mbs/wilderness/alakes

Bellevue Parks: www.ci.bellevue.wa.us/parks

Bellingham Parks: 360/676-6985; www.cob.org/parks

Capitol State Forest: 800/527-3305

Department of Natural Resources, South Puget Sound Region: 360/825-1631

Issaquah Alps Trails Club: 206/328-0480; www.issaquahalps.org

King County Parks: 206/296-4232; www.metrokc.gov/parks

Mount Baker–Snoqualmie National Forest: www.fs.fed.us/r6/mbs

Mount Rainier National Park: 360/569-2211; www.nps.gov/mora

Mount St. Helens National Volcanic Monument: 360/247-3955; www.fs.fed/us/gpnf/mshnvm

North Cascades National Park: www.nps.gov/noca

Olympic National Park: 360/452-4501; www.nps.gov/olym

Seattle Parks: 206/684-4075; www.ci.seattle.wa.us/parks

Snohomish County Parks: 425/388-6600; www.co.snohomish.wa.us/parks

Tacoma Parks: 253/305-1000; www.ci.tacoma.wa.us/parks

Washington State Parks: 800/233-0321; www.parks.wa.gov

Whatcom County Parks: 360/733-2900; www.co.whatcom.wa.us/parks

Running Clubs

Cascade Running Club
P.O. Box 218
Kirkland, WA 98083-218
www.pws.prserv.net/CascadeRunningClub

Club Northwest
206/633-4872
www.cnw.org

Eastside Runners
P.O. Box 2616
Redmond, WA 98073-2616
www.eastsiderunners.com

Ft. Steilacoom Running Club
F.S.R.C.
P.O. BOX 1726
Tacoma, WA 98401
www.ontherun.com/fsrcidx.htm

Greater Bellingham Running Club
P.O. Box 683
Bellingham, WA 98227
360/734-3953 or 360/595-2403
www.ontherun.com/gbrcclub.htm

Interurban Runners Club
www.ontherun.com/clubs/irc

North Sound Runners
Marysville, WA
425/397-7214
rtown22@aol.com

Skagit Runners
Burlington, WA
360/757-1781
cessil@aol.com

Team SSR
3409 Capitol Blvd
Olympia, WA 98501
360/705-2580
www.southsoundrunning.com/Home.htm

Washington State Ultra-Distance Trail Running, Walking, and Duathlon Club
P.O. Box 39623
Tacoma, WA 98439
www.trifind.com/humansports

Web Sites

www.ontherun.com: A great site in and of itself. Click on links page for a seemingly endless supply of running links around the world.

www.mountainrunning.com: Offers trail running information for Canada and the world.

www.runtheplanet.com: Touts itself as the largest worldwide running community on the Internet.

www.trailrunner.com: The American Trail Running Association. Promotes trail and mountain running.

www.fox.nstn.ca/~dblaikie: Ultramarathon World, a resource for athletes who run farther than marathon distance (26.2 miles).

Magazines

Northwest Runner (www.runningnetwork.com/nwrunner)

Trail Runner (www.trailrunnermag.com)

Ultra Running (www.ultrarunning.com)

Runner's World (www.runnersworld.com)

Trailwork Opportunities

Take some time to help out with those trails you love to run. Here are some organizations that offer plenty of opportunities:

Washington Trails Association: www.wta.org

The Volunteer Trailwork Coalition: www.trailwork.org

Race Calendar

JANUARY

Bridle Trails Twilight 50K
Kirkland, WA
425/828-0250
cdralph@attglobal.net
www.pws.prserv.net/CascadeRunningClub/
bt50k.htm

Fat Ass 50K
Tiger Mountain
Issaquah, WA
ronn@wdfenet.com

FEBRUARY

Mazama Snowshoe Shuffle 10K/5K/2K
Twisp, WA
509/996-3287
www.mvsta.com

MARCH

Chuckanut Mountain 50K
Bellingham, WA
360/671-5978
www.basecampwa.com/chuckanut50K

APRIL

Mount Si Relay & Ultra Run (50 miles)
Snoqualmie, WA
877/242-1634
www.ontherun.com/mtsirelay

McDonald Forest 50K
Corvalis, OR
541/737-2373
www.orst.edu/groups/triclub/ultra/ultra.html

Peace Park Trail Run (5 miles)
Janeville, BC
608/756-1832

MAY

Sunflower Relay and Iron Event
Twisp, WA
509/996-3287
www.mvsta.com

JUNE

Ultra-Man Trail Run/Walk (5K to 50K)
Lakewood, WA
253/376-0092
humansports2001@hotmail.com

Sun Mountain Trail Run (5 & 10 miles)
Twisp, WA
509/996-3287
www.mvsta.com

Adidas Five Peaks Series
Vancouver, BC
604/572-4625
www.fivepeaks.com

JULY

Chuckanut Foot Race (7 miles)
Bellingham, WA
360/734-3953

Daybreak Climb a Mountain (34.3 miles)
Spokane, WA
509/927-1688
www.daybreakrun.org

White River Trail Run 50 Miler
Greenwater, WA
206/488-7178
www.pws.prserv.net/CascadeRunningClub

Knee Knackering North Shore Trail Run (50K)
West Vancouver, BC
604/222-3199
www.kneeknacker.com

AUGUST

Cutthroat Classic (12 Miles)
Mazama, WA
509/996-3287
www.mvsta.com

Cascade Crest Classic 100 Mile
Easton, WA
509/656-260
randyg@eburg.com

Super Energy XC (5K to 20K)
Lakewood, WA
253/376-0092
www.trifind.com/humansports

PCT at Mount Hood (50 Mile/50 K)
Portland, OR
503/439-0799
www.orrc.net

Adidas Five Peaks Series
Vancouver, BC
604/572-4625
www.fivepeaks.com

SEPTEMBER

Cle Elum Ridge Trail Run (50K)
Cle Elum, WA
206/525-1295
seafrank@seanet.com

Plain Endurance Run (100 Miles)
Plain, WA
www.pws.prserv.net/CascadeRunningClub/
plain.htm

Adidas Five Peaks Series
Vancouver, BC
604/572-4625
www.fivepeaks.com

NOVEMBER

Ron Herzog Memorial 50k
Granite Falls, WA
425/828-0250
cdralph@attglobal.net
www.pws/prserv.net/CascadeRunningClub

Dances with Turkeys Trail Run 5K, 10K, 15K
Lakewood, WA
253/376-009
humansports2001@hotmailcom
www.trifind.com/humansports

Adventure Run 10K Trail Run
St. Edward State Park
Kenmore, WA
206/271-0652

DECEMBER

Midnight Express Trail 8K
Lakewood, WA
253/376-009
humansports2001@hotmailcom
www.trifind.com/humansports

Geographical Index

Anacortes area
  Heart Lake-Mount Erie Loop, 31
  Whistle Lake, 35
Baker Lake, 50
Bellevue area
  Cougar Mountain Ring, 93
  Mercer Slough Nature Park, 88
  Squak Mountain Loop, 97
Bellingham area
  Blanchard Mountain Loop, 22
  Chuckanut Ridge-Lost Lake Loop, 18
  Hemlock Trail/Raptor Ridge, 14
  Lake Padden, 11
  Lookout Mountain Intestine, 7
  Lookout Mountain Towers, 4
  North Lake Whatcom, 1
  Squires Lake/Alger Mountain, 25
Blanchard Mountain Loop, 22
Camp Sheppard-Forest Shelter Loop, 150
Capitol Peak, 140
Cascade Lake Loop, 63
Cascade Pass-Sahale Arm, 53
Chain Lakes Loop, 43
Chuckanut Ridge-Lost Lake Loop, 18
Cougar Mountain Ring, 93
Discovery Park Loop, 82
Elk Mountain, 156
Everett area
  Mount Pilchuck, 69
  Spencer Island, 66
Hannegan Peak, 39
Heart Lake-Mount Erie Loop, 31
Hemlock Trail/Raptor Ridge, 14
Highway 2 (Stevens Pass)

Iron Goat Trail, 75
Wallace Falls State Park, 72
Highway 20
  Baker Lake, 50
  Cascade Pass-Sahale Arm, 53
  Scott Paul Trail, 47
I-90 (Snoqualmie Pass)
  Cougar Mountain Ring, 93
  Kendall Katwalk, 131
  Melakwa & Pratt Lakes Loop, 127
  Mount Si, 117
  Rattlesnake Mountain, 120
  Snoqualmie Valley Trail, 124
  South & Middle Tiger, 108
  Squak Mountain Loop, 97
  Tiger Mountain 6/12 Summits, 113
  West Tiger 3, 101
  West Tiger Three-Summit Loop, 104
  Wilderness Peak Loop, 90
Ipsut Creek-Spray Park Loop, 146
Iron Goat Trail, 75
Issaquah area
  Cougar Mountain Ring, 93
  Rattlesnake Mountain, 120
  South & Middle Tiger, 108
  Squak Mountain Loop, 97
  Tiger Mountain 6/12 Summits, 113
  West Tiger 3, 101
  West Tiger Three-Summit Loop, 104
  Wilderness Peak Loop, 90
Kendall Katwalk, 131
Lake Padden, 11
Little Mountain, 28
Lookout Mountain Intestine, 7
Lookout Mountain Towers, 4
Loowit Trail, 167
Margaret McKenny Loop, 137
Mercer Slough Nature Park, 88

Melakwa & Pratt Lakes Loop, 127
Millersylvania State Park, 143
Mountain Lake to Mount Constitution, 56
Mount Baker Highway
    Chain Lakes Loop, 43
    Hannegan Peak, 39
Mount Constitution/Pickett Loop, 59
Mount Pilchuck, 69
Mount Rainier
    Camp Sheppard-Forest Shelter Loop, 150
    Ipsut Creek-Spray Park Loop, 146
    Wonderland to Panhandle Gap, 153
Mount Si, 117
Mount St. Helens
    Loowit Trail, 167
Mount Vernon area
    Little Mountain, 28
North Lake Whatcom, 1
Olympia area
    Capitol Peak, 140
    Margaret McKenny Loop, 137
    Millersylvania State Park, 143
Olympic Peninsula
    Elk Mountain, 156
    Ozette Trails, 163
    Spruce Railroad Trail, 160
Ozette Trails, 163
Point Defiance Park, 134
Rattlesnake Mountain, 120
San Juan Islands
    Cascade Lake Loop, 63
    Mountain Lake to Mount Constitution, 56
    Mount Constitution/Pickett Loop, 59
Scott Paul Trail, 47
Seattle area
    Discovery Park Loop, 82
    St. Edward State Park, 79
    Washington Park Arboretum, 85

Snoqualmie Valley Trail, 124
South & Middle Tiger, 108
Spencer Island, 66
Spruce Railroad Trail, 160
Squak Mountain Loop, 97
Squires Lake/Alger Mountain, 25
St. Edward State Park, 79
Tacoma area
    Point Defiance Park, 134
Tiger Mountain
    South & Middle Tiger, 108
    Tiger Mountain 6/12 Summits, 113
    West Tiger 3, 10
    West Tiger Three-Summit Loop, 104
Wallace Falls State Park, 72
Washington Park Arboretum, 85
West Tiger 3, 10
West Tiger Three-Summit Loop, 104
Whistle Lake, 35
Wilderness Peak Loop, 90
Wonderland to Panhandle Gap, 153

Runs by Pain
(Difficulty)

🏃

Cascade Lake Loop, 63
Discovery Park Loop, 82
Lake Padden, 11
Mercer Slough Nature Park, 88
Millersylvania State Park, 143
North Lake Whatcom, 1
Point Defiance Park, 134
Spencer Island, 66
Washington Park Arboretum, 85

🏃🏃

Cougar Mountain Ring, 93
Iron Goat Trail, 75
Little Mountain, 28
Lookout Mountain Intestine, 7
Lookout Mountain Towers, 4
Margaret McKenny Loop, 137
Ozette Trails, 163
Snoqualmie Valley Trail, 124
Spruce Railroad Trail, 160
Squires Lake/Alger Mountain, 25
St. Edward State Park, 79
Whistle Lake, 35
Wilderness Peak Loop, 90

🏃🏃🏃

Baker Lake, 50
Blanchard Mountain Loop, 22
Capitol Peak, 140
Chain Lakes Loop, 43

Chuckanut Ridge-Lost Lake Loop, 18
Heart Lake-Mount Erie Loop, 31
Hemlock Trail/Raptor Ridge, 14
Mountain Lake to Mount Constitution, 56
Mount Pilchuck, 69
Rattlesnake Mountain, 120
Scott Paul Trail, 47
South & Middle Tiger, 108
Squak Mountain Loop, 97
Wallace Falls State Park, 72
West Tiger 3, 101

🏃🏃🏃🏃

Camp Sheppard-Forest Shelter Loop, 150
Hannegan Peak, 39
Kendall Katwalk, 131
Mount Constitution/Pickett Loop, 56
West Tiger Three-Summit Loop, 104
Wonderland to Panhandle Gap, 153

🏃🏃🏃🏃🏃

Cascade Pass-Sahale Arm, 53
Elk Mountain, 156
Ipsut Creek-Spray Park Loop, 146
Loowit Trail, 167
Melakwa & Pratt Lakes Loop, 127
Mount Si, 117
Tiger Mountain 6/12 Summits, 113

Runs by Gain
(Fun Factor & Aesthetic Appeal)

Hemlock Trail/Raptor Ridge, 14
Iron Goat Trail, 75
Little Mountain, 28
Lookout Mountain Towers, 4
Lookout Mountain Intestine, 7
Margaret McKenny Loop, 137
North Lake Whatcom, 1
Rattlesnake Mountain, 120
South & Middle Tiger, 108
Spruce Railroad Trail, 160
Squak Mountain Loop, 97
Squires Lake/Alger Mountain, 25
West Tiger 3, 101
West Tiger Three–Summit Loop, 104
Whistle Lake, 35

Cascade Pass–Sahale Arm, 53
Chain Lakes Loop, 43
Elk Mountain, 156
Hannegan Peak, 39
Ipsut Creek–Spray Park Loop, 146
Loowit Trail, 167
Melakwa & Pratt Lakes Loop, 127
Mountain Lake to Mount Constitution, 56
Ozette Trails, 163
Scott Paul Trail, 47
Wonderland to Panhandle Gap, 46

Cascade Lake Loop, 63
Lake Padden, 11
Mercer Slough Nature Park, 88
Millersylvania State Park, 143
Point Defiance Park, 134
Snoqualmie Valley Trail, 124
Spencer Island, 66
St. Edward State Park, 79
Washington Park Arboretum, 85
Wilderness Peak Loop, 90

Camp Sheppard–Forest Shelter Loop, 150
Capitol Peak, 140
Kendall Katwalk, 131
Mount Constitution/Pickett Loop, 56
Mount Pilchuck, 69
Mount Si, 117
Tiger Mountain 6/12 Summits, 113
Wallace Falls State Park, 72

Baker Lake, 50
Blanchard Mountain Loop, 22
Chuckanut Ridge–Lost Lake Loop, 18
Cougar Mountain Ring, 93
Discovery Park Loop, 82
Heart Lake–Mount Erie Loop, 31

About the Author

Mike McQuaide is a freelance writer and former outdoor recreation reporter for the *Bellingham Herald* and Gannett News Service. His articles have appeared in numerous regional and national publications, including *Trail Runner*, *Runner's World*, *Northwest Runner*, *Seattle Post-Intelligencer*, and *USA Today*. A veteran of Northwest trails for more than a dozen years, McQuaide is also an avid mountaineer, snowboarder, cyclist, and baseball player. He lives in Bellingham with his wife and young son, Baker.